From Intention to Impact

Management on the Cutting Edge series

Abbie Lundberg, series editor

Published in cooperation with *MIT Sloan Management Review*

Marco Bertini and Oded Koenigsberg, *The Ends Game: How Smart Companies Stop Selling Products and Start Delivering Value*

Christian Stadler, Julia Hautz, Kurt Matzler, and Stephan Friedrich von den Eichen, *Open Strategy: Mastering Disruption from Outside the C-Suite*

Gerald Kane, Rich Nanda, Anh Nguyen Phillips, and Jonathan Copulsky, *The Transformation Myth: Leading Your Organization through Uncertain Times*

Ron Adner, *Winning the Right Game: How to Disrupt, Defend, and Deliver in a Changing World*

Satish Nambisan and Yadong Luo, *The Digital Multinational: Navigating the New Normal in Global Business*

Ravin Jesuthasan and John W. Boudreau, *Work without Jobs: How to Reboot Your Organization's Work Operating System*

Mohan Subramaniam, *The Future of Competitive Strategy: Unleashing the Power of Data and Digital Ecosystems*

Chris B. Bingham and Rory M. McDonald, *Productive Tensions: How Every Leader Can Tackle Innovation's Toughest Trade-Offs*

Thomas H. Davenport and Steven M. Miller, *Working with AI: Real Stories of Human-Machine Collaboration*

Ravi Sarathy, *Enterprise Strategy for Blockchain: Lessons in Disruption from Fintech, Supply Chains, and Consumer Industries*

Lynda Gratton, *Redesigning Work: How to Transform Your Organization and Make Hybrid Work for Everyone*

John Horn, *Inside the Competitor's Mindset: How to Predict Their Next Move and Position Yourself for Success*

Elizabeth J. Altman, David Kiron, Jeff Schwartz, and Robin Jones, *Workforce Ecosystems: Reaching Strategic Goals with People, Partners, and Technologies*

Barbara H. Wixom, Cynthia M. Beath, and Leslie Owens, *Data Is Everybody's Business: The Fundamentals of Data Monetization*

Eric Siegel, *The AI Playbook: Mastering the Rare Art of Machine Learning Deployment*

Malia C. Lazu, *From Intention to Impact: A Practical Guide to Diversity, Equity, and Inclusion*

Daniel Aronson, *The Value of Values: The Hidden Superpower That Drives Business and Career Success*

MITSloan
Management Review

From Intention to Impact

A Practical Guide to Diversity, Equity, and Inclusion

Malia C. Lazu

The MIT Press
Cambridge, Massachusetts
London, England

The MIT Press would like to thank the anonymous peer reviewers who provided comments on drafts of this book. The generous work of academic experts is essential for establishing the authority and quality of our publications. We acknowledge with gratitude the contributions of these otherwise uncredited readers.

This book was set in Stone Serif and Stone Sans by Jen Jackowitz. Printed and bound in the United States of America.

Library of Congress Cataloging-in-Publication Data

Names: Lazu, Malia C., author.
Title: From intention to impact : a practical guide to diversity, equity, and
    inclusion / Malia C. Lazu.
Description: Cambridge, Massachusetts : The MIT Press, [2024] | Series:
    Management on the cutting edge series | Includes bibliographical
    references and index.
Identifiers: LCCN 2023012166 (print) | LCCN 2023012167 (ebook) | ISBN
    9780262048842 (hardcover) | ISBN 9780262377898 (epub) | ISBN
    9780262377881 (pdf)
Subjects: LCSH: Social responsibility of business. | Anti-racism. | Racial justice.
Classification: LCC HD60 .L398 2024 (print) | LCC HD60 (ebook) | DDC
    658.4/08—dc23/eng/20230907
LC record available at https://lccn.loc.gov/2023012166
LC ebook record available at https://lccn.loc.gov/2023012167

10 9 8 7 6 5 4 3 2 1

To all those—past, present, and future—
who are dedicated to expanding justice, everywhere

Contents

Series Foreword   ix

Introduction   xi

I   **How We Got Here**   1

    1   **Waking Up to Uncomfortable Truths**   3

    2   **Evolve or Die**   11

    3   **Making Antiracism the New Normal**   27

II   **A Blueprint for Sustainable Change**   41

    4   **From Performative Action to Business Performance**   43

    5   **Finding Your Company's Authentic Voice**   57

    6   **Goals Alone Do Not Make Change—Uninformed Goals Pose a Reputational Risk**   67

    7   **Creating a Curious Work Culture**   83

    8   **It's Not Them, It's You**   105

    9   **Vendor Procurement: Building Diverse Ecosystems**   119

    10   **Where to from Here?**   129

Acknowledgments   139

Notes   141

Index   159

Series Foreword

The world does not lack for management ideas. Thousands of researchers, practitioners, and other experts produce tens of thousands of articles,
books, papers, posts, and podcasts each year. But only a scant few promise
to truly move the needle on practice, and fewer still dare to reach into
the future of what management will become. It is this rare breed of idea—
meaningful to practice, grounded in evidence, and *built for the future*—that
we seek to present in this series.

Abbie Lundberg
Editor in chief
MIT Sloan Management Review

Introduction

> There is no single face in nature, because every eye that looks upon it, sees it from
> its own angle. So every man's spice-box seasons his own food.
> —Zora Neale Hurston

The year 2022 marked a first for corporate awareness of Juneteenth, a newly adopted federal holiday now on the calendar in the wake of police killings of black people, including George Floyd. I wasn't expecting much from corporations—but this! It seemed like a *Saturday Night Live* skit: red-velvet-and-cheesecake-flavored ice cream being sold at Walmart to celebrate the emancipation of black bodies from being sold. Could a company be so clueless as to sell cartons of Great Value Celebration ice cream in packaging adorned with the pan-African colors of red, black, green, and yellow and with cartoon-style hands making peace signs and giving high-fives, surrounded by musical notes? Printed on the side was the goal of producing, buying, and consuming this ice cream: to "share and celebrate African American culture, emancipation and enduring hope."

The social media backlash was swift and intense, and an apologetic Walmart pulled the ice cream from its freezers amid stinging accusations that it had tried to commercialize a holiday that commemorates the end of slavery in America. In its statement, Walmart acknowledged that "a few items [being sold for Juneteenth] caused concern for some of our customers and we sincerely apologize."[1] This wasn't the first time Walmart got it wrong where the BIPOC—Black, Indigenous, and people of color—community was concerned. In 2021, Walmart faced a proposed nationwide class action suit that held that the company, the largest private employer in the United States, discriminated against black and Latinx job applicants by imposing stricter background checks on them, and failed to take rehabilitation and other circumstances into consideration.[2] Especially on top of such allegations of bias, Walmart's selling Juneteenth ice cream was tone-deaf and insensitive. In retrospect, Walmart would have been far better off partnering with Creamalicious, a black-owned ice cream brand that makes a red velvet cheesecake flavor as part of its Southern-inspired ice cream offerings.

Instead, Walmart set itself up for the kind of marketing mess that happens when people of color either are not in the room or feel it is not safe to speak up with their honest opinions. But when the corporate apology comes out, you have to wonder: *What were they thinking?*

In the wake of the May 2022 Tops grocery store mass shooting in Buffalo, New York, an egregious act carried out in the name of white supremacy, the 2022 commemoration of Juneteenth took on even greater meaning, and not only in the black community but across America. Juneteenth is a solemn commemoration of the day in 1865 when a group of enslaved people in Texas were finally allowed to leave their plantation free. Although the Emancipation Proclamation had been issued on January 1, 1863, the spread of the news and the doctrine depended on how far the Union troops were able to advance in the face of the Confederacy's relentless refusal to give up an economic system that required the enslavement of people. It should also be noted that there is not shared agreement on how Juneteenth should be interpreted. Some do not believe we should center the Union leader but rather the continued occupation of a supposedly free people. As Henry Louis Gates of Harvard University said in his op-ed piece in the *Bay State Banner*, "Hardly the recipe for a celebration—which is what makes the story of 'Juneteenth' all the more remarkable. Defying confusion and delay, terror and violence, the newly 'freed' Black men and women of Texas, with the aid of the Freedmen's Bureau (itself delayed from arriving until September 1865), now had a date to rally around. In one of the most inspiring grassroots efforts of the post–Civil War period, they transformed June 19 from a day of unheeded military orders into their own annual rite, 'Juneteenth,' beginning one year later in 1866."[3] The first Juneteenth celebrations were recorded in Texas in 1866, and observations of the day spread throughout the South in the 1920s and 1930s. That Juneteenth is now a national holiday is a victory of sorts, but also a cautionary moment—a window into the much larger issues of systemic racism, white ignorance, and white fragility in America.

Juneteenth needs to be more than just a day off work—or a reason to have a sale or feature a "special" product. Far more important is asking ourselves how this moment should be honored and observed as part of both black history and the uncomfortable chapters of American history that span both the enslavement and the current liberation of black people. Otherwise Juneteenth runs the risk of being discounted, gradually losing its meaning as it becomes commercialized by marketers as a hook for their product campaigns. Equally damaging, the observance of Juneteenth by corporations could be reduced to an exercise in blackwashing to check some box on their environmental, social, and governance (ESG) scorecards—as happens with so much of their attempts at diversity, equity, and inclusion (DEI) work.

Such risks of cultural appropriation are all too real and already experienced by many groups. My gay friends, for instance, talk with mixed feelings about how Pride has gone mainstream. Yes, it does make it easier to raise funds for good causes, but Pride symbols on corporate websites and products would not necessarily be the first thing the gay community would have asked for, especially at a time when so many nonbinary and transgender individuals still face inequality and a lack of acceptance.

Let's assume that Walmart had the best intentions when it stocked its freezers with this ice cream. The retailer no doubt envisioned people going to Juneteenth barbecues and buying Juneteenth ice cream to celebrate the black community's endurance and not being chattel anymore. But as my grandma always reminded me, the road to hell is paved with good intentions. Every time corporate America gets it wrong, the strategy loses its ability to have impact.

The business community continues to fall in the gap between intention and impact, and all too often finds itself needing to pull a product or issue an apology—a significant cost in terms of money and reputation. Corporate America has to do better because America is asking it to do better.

* * *

I am an Afro Puerto Rican Italian woman who was born and raised in Honolulu, Hawaii.

When I was a child, I received my first book on black history, given to me by my father's girlfriend. Looking back, what I remember most was that the book was actually a photocopy—that's how inaccessible black education was. This was decades before Ibram X. Kendi's *Antiracist Baby* would hit the shelves and be vilified by Senator Ted Cruz (R-Texas) during the Supreme Court nomination hearings for Justice Ketanji Brown Jackson. Back then, all I had were those photocopied pages to help me understand my identity.

Within the black community there are countless personal stories like mine, stories of self-discovery and of grappling with what it means to be a person of color in America. Individually and collectively, we have spent decades uncovering and discovering, from mourning tragic events to celebrating our heritage with enduring hope, and often through stories outside the mainstream narrative.

My professional journey started as a community organizer. I have also been a business owner and even a bank president. At each juncture of my career, I have let the community know I was going into my new role with all of them in my mind and on my heart. I signaled that as a new bank president in 2019 with an op-ed column I wrote for the *Boston Globe*, appropriately titled "Going Corporate for a Cause." As I wrote at the time, "In this political and economic climate, I believe that 'going corporate' to help people makes perfect sense. As an old hand in public advocacy, I am hopeful that community banking will help get valuable capital flowing downstream so that all of us, and I really mean all of us, can thrive."[4] Those words are even truer today for me as I work "on the inside" with corporations, particularly in financial services and commercial real estate.

Grassroots Activist

In 2003, when I was twenty-six years old, I was introduced to Harry Belafonte. Born in Harlem, of Jamaican descent, he was part of the West Indian community, as reflected in his music. The recipient of three Grammy Awards, as well as historic Emmy and Tony Awards, and a Rock & Roll Hall of Fame inductee, Belafonte also was honored for his social activism, including being awarded the Ford Foundation's Freedom Medal. Among those in his circle were Rev. Dr. Martin Luther King Jr. and singer-activist Paul Robeson. He supported causes from ending apartheid in South Africa to juvenile justice reform in the United States. These were the reasons we began working together—me, a young social activist, and Belafonte, who always supported freedom movements.

With his passing in April 2023, Belafonte left a legacy that shaped how thousands of younger activists—myself included—do their work. He will always be the one who modeled what he believed.

Looking back, I recall that I started working with Belafonte in earnest after he had seen an image that he could not shake and that would catalyze his activism for years to come. It was a picture of a six-year-old black girl getting arrested. In that moment he realized that, despite all the work he had done—he had been blacklisted in the 1950s for being politically outspoken—there was so much more left to do. Here was a child who clearly had done nothing wrong other than act out in school. Instead of calling her mother, school officials decided to call the police. Belafonte was committed to changing the status quo and believed it started at the grass roots, through giving youth greater opportunity and a sense of belonging.

Being an activist was what I was born to do. When I was an undergraduate at Emerson College in the 1990s, I started a nonprofit called Mass VOTE in hopes of changing voting culture in Massachusetts. At that time, I had not planned on becoming a community organizer, but soon I would discover just how much this suited me: bringing people together to help them find and own their power.

When I was hired by Belafonte to work in marginalized communities to reduce youth violence, I eagerly embraced this work. To have an impact, I needed to learn much more about the deeper roots of violence in these communities, in particular the role of gangs in generating sources of revenue in places where other economic opportunities and resources are few and far between. When people don't have access to legitimate work and financing, they will turn to underground economies, often based in illegal transactions. Little did I know at the outset that this work would help me identify how calcified systems maintain the status quo of inequity and what it takes to shift those systems. What I learned working with Belafonte would shape the course of my work in DEI forever.

Belafonte founded the Gathering of the Elders (now known as the Gathering for Justice), which brought together civil rights leaders such as Diane Nash, Bob Moses, and Rev. Al Sharpton. From the beginning, the Gathering was conceived as a safe space for dialogue among activists, street organizations, academics, community members, and formerly incarcerated people. The Gathering also received support and models of activism from many organizations, including the Student Nonviolent Coordinating Committee, the NAACP, the Southern Christian Leadership Conference, and the Congress on Racial Equality.[5]

Out of the Gathering of the Elders came a plan for a series of youth meetings across the country. It was to be a cross-cultural experience—country meeting city, North meeting South—and a reaching out to youth who had been involved with gangs or criminal activity. What transpired was eye-opening and life-changing as connections were forged group to group, person to person. It was one of the most formative experiences of my life and forged my path as a social activist—a role I maintain to this day, including in my DEI consulting work.

Belafonte understood that we needed to first organize the community so youth could get to know each other. Helping to engender a deeper sense of commonality and connection, Belafonte believed, was the first step toward interrupting the violent economies that are offered to youth in marginalized communities. Instead of just rushing in with solutions and answers, we had to understand more about what this community needed. We listened and learned before we took action.

This is an important takeaway for corporate leaders today: invest the time to listen, especially to people within your communities—and that starts with employees. Don't just do a survey and decide that a few points and clicks can tell the full truth of what it is like to be a person of color within your organization. Listen and learn in a way that builds trust and makes it safe for others to speak their truth. Otherwise the need to do something will negate the need to do something impactful.

Working with Belafonte, our first outreach involved taking black youth from the North to the South, bridging regional divides to find common ground and encourage dialogue. At the end of this gathering, we had the genesis of a youth movement. To keep up the momentum of the listening tour, we took a cross section of the black youth to Northern California to meet with Latino kids. It could have been a culture clash, but in the end, commonalities prevailed. I recall overhearing two of the young people talking to each other: "These folks are cool." "Their rice and beans are good, too."

From there we went to the Onondaga Nation in Syracuse, New York, to bring Indigenous youth into the dialogue. For the black and Hispanic youth—some of whom had never been on an airplane before—it was an incredible opportunity to visit a Native American community and hear of their experiences. The Onondaga people told us how they had lost their lands and had pledged to become nonviolent by burying their guns in the 1970s during the American Indian Movement. The youth listened with rapt attention as the Onondagas explained a confrontation with the National Guard in the 1970s when the Onondaga people, men, women, and children, lined up on the border of their land to keep the guardsmen from entering. Learning from one another broke down racial and cultural barriers, and these young people started seeing their commonalities.

In Los Angeles, black, brown, Indigenous, and white kids met with Asian youth. A lot of stereotypes were broken as our youth learned that the lifestyles of their Asian peers were not all that different from their own. From there we took our kids to Appalachia, where many of them mingled with poor whites for the first time. These urban kids had never seen anything like rural Kentucky and West Virginia, where water was pumped by hand from a well.

Seeing this, one of our young people of color got angry and accused me of lying to him. When I asked him to explain, he said, "You tell us that if we work hard and come together, we'll get ahead. But look at how George Bush treats his own people. That means we'll never get ahead."

At the time, Kentucky was the site of a new super-maximum security "supermax" prison. We wanted the kids, many of whom lived in neighborhoods where joining a gang provided the most reliable way to earn money for their families, to see what the other consequences of gang membership could be. But that's not the only lesson learned while we were in Appalachia. The supermax had been sold to the community as a project that would create jobs, but the incidence of domestic violence and alcoholism exploded as Appalachian residents became guards and overseers in the prison system. It was yet another example of violence begetting violence. And yet there were black and brown kids, dancing at a hootenanny with the kids from Appalachia, affirming their shared humanity. More borders and barriers were being broken down. Getting to know each other helped the young people from varied backgrounds understand their interconnectedness, including how inequity not only negatively affects those being oppressed but also hurts those with privilege.

In his autobiographical *Narrative of the Life of Frederick Douglass an American Slave*, Douglass wrote how his once-kind mistress had changed. "But, alas! This kind heart had but a short time to remain such. The fatal poison of irresponsible power was already in her hands, and soon commenced its infernal work. That cheerful eye, under the influence of slavery, soon became red with rage; that voice, made all of sweet accord, changed to one of harsh and horrid discord; and that angelic face gave place to that of a demon."[6] Today the poison of white supremacy still flows: overtly in the commission of hate crimes and covertly in the omission of people of color from positions of power at the top of organizations in corporate America. No one is spared its insidiousness.

A Pilgrimage to Nonviolence

Finally, after two years of work, our efforts culminated in 1,500 youths from twenty-six states coming together in Oakland. Belafonte had the foresight to tell Hilton security that he would not tolerate these youth being judged, and I wonder if that was the reason there were no problems. Everyone was treated with respect, so they acted with respect. The worst things that happened on the trip was one kid got ripped off when he went out to buy weed, and a sixteen-year-old couple were caught "fooling around" in one of the hotel rooms. Peacefully, we walked out of the Hilton accompanied

by supporters, including the actors Alan Alda and Danny Glover. That was the kind presence Harry could inspire.

Most important, the youth at the gathering pledged allegiance to nonviolence, which kicked off training for more than three thousand youth in the six principles of Kingian nonviolence as defined by Dr. King in his "A Pilgrimage to Nonviolence" essay. Among the principles: "Nonviolence is a way of life for courageous people."[7]

Out of this initiative came the realization that these youth needed to have economic alternatives to dealing drugs or engaging in sex work or trafficking guns. Father Greg Boyle, a Catholic priest who founded Homeboy Industries, the world's largest gang intervention program, based in Los Angeles, was one of our elders. We wanted to build on his work in creating a model of helping that leveraged the gang ecosystem. That led us to help youth start businesses in several cities around the country.

During this work of helping kids start businesses, I had an epiphany. As wonderful as it was to support entrepreneurship and small-business ownership, those efforts needed to be integrated into the mainstream economy. I recognized that this is the role of business in our liberation and in our walk to achieve equity for people of color. And this is the work I am still doing today—different in form, but the same in substance: I am an activist working closely with and in the business community.

As I wrote in that opinion column published in the *Boston Globe*, "My two decades of community work highlighted how capitalist structures often leave behind so many people. But I was fighting from the outside, and that limited my impact."[8] I am still a social activist, but I'm working with and within companies to catalyze change. By combining my experiences from the grass roots to the C-suite, I draw on a unique background in writing this book.

Over twenty-plus years spent in many different positions, I have worked to level the playing field and build power within communities so that intentions can become impactful. Through my work I have had the honor of getting to know some of the most ignored groups in America. What I see again and again—whether in the Mississippi Delta or on the fortieth floor corporate headquarters—is that until America, including companies, learns how to value the talent and contributions of people of color, racial equity will not be achievable.

Over the last ten years, I have taken these observations and experiences into my work with corporations and organizations. I have seen what it takes to ensure that the DEI intentions you, corporate leaders, seek to promote racial equity have an actual impact on your business.

The value to be recognized is not just economic but also social and cultural. Think about the contributions of individuals from Harriet Tubman to George Washington Carver, from Jimi Hendrix to Cesar Chavez, and on to Katherine Johnson and the other black women trailblazers at NASA, entertainment icons such as Issa Rae and Questlove, the Academy Award–winning filmmaker of *Summer of Soul*, a movie set in the summer of 1969—"a paradigm shift moment where . . . civil rights is ending and Black Power is starting."[9]

A Time for Systems Change

The best time for systems change is when systems are failing. That's why now is the right time to shift culture and create systems that can respond to a twenty-first-century context. Explicitly, this century is a time of generational realignment and acknowledgment of systems failure. To quote youth climate change leader Greta Thunberg, "We don't want these things to be done by 2050, 2030 or even 2021, we want this done now—as in *right now*."[10]

As I discuss in detail throughout this book, George Floyd's murder was a wake-up call. In the aftermath, corporations doubled down on their public intentions to be more inclusive and equitable. Yet beyond the pledges and promises, it's hard to see the system changes that need to be made to result in impact. This is the case for a few reasons. First, people don't actually know where we are starting from with equity, never mind how to get to where they want to be. Second, changes to systems are hard to do when you are busy using those systems to make money. Sadly, we are already seeing retreat from the commitments made after George Floyd.

That's why DEI work seems hard on the best day and impossible on the worst—because moving from intention to impact means changing the traditions and culture that normalize whiteness. Like anything else that's done unconsciously, white-centric actions feel natural in corporate America. But this blindness to bias makes changing whiteness almost impossible. "Imagine an ignorance that resists, that fights back," race theorist Charles Mills writes in his essay "White Ignorance."[11] There is a core belief held by many Americans that this system can work for everyone, if everyone will just try hard enough. White ignorance assumes that everyone has access to opportunity, without ever thinking about how systemic bias plays a role in determining who has the access they need to succeed.

In her book, *How to Be Less Stupid about Race*, Crystal M. Fleming writes, "Race is a fundamentally stupid idea" that continues to define human beings as fundamentally different and unequal in abilities, both physical and mental. This unscientific categorization feeds domination based on race, resulting in racist beliefs about the supposed natural superiority of one race over another and superficial beliefs about racial order.[12]

As a result of this racial stupidity, many people may assume that DEI work means checking boxes, lowering standards, or, to be really blunt, playing favorites with women and people of color—all the while ignoring the plethora of data highlighting the overall benefits to company profitability from increasing diversity. Without question, centering whiteness carries a heavy economic cost.

The International Monetary Fund (IMF) observed that, in the United States, racism has stymied black economic progress for decades. Examples abound, such as denying most soldiers of color access to the benefits of the GI Bill, which propelled growth for the rest of the American middle class. The reason? Opposition from white congressmen from the South who clung to racial segregation. Redlining became the shorthand for Federal Housing Administration policy that refused insurance for mortgages on houses in black neighborhoods, effectively shutting black Americans out of home ownership and the means to accumulate wealth by owning property.[13]

As the McKinsey Institute for Black Economic Mobility has observed: "There is a wide and persistent gap in wealth between white and black families."[14] However, efforts to close the racial wealth gap would result in the U.S. GDP being 4 to 6 percent higher by 2028, resulting in more economic opportunity for all.[15] It's also a global issue, as the IMF report clearly shows. For example, in France, creating equality in access to employment and education could help boost that country's GDP by 1.5 percent over the next twenty years, representing a $3.6 billion economic bonus.[16] To capture this value in every country, the onus of change where systemic racism is concerned must be placed on every institution, across education, health care, criminal justice, culture, sports and entertainment, and, of course, businesses in every economic sector.

For years, employers have heard the calls to change their narrative around DEI and social justice. Many have jumped on the ESG bandwagon, but with far more enthusiasm for the "E" (environment) and with producing evidence of their "G" (governance), while glossing over the "S" because, frankly, social change is hard to do.

Engaging in DEI efforts means taking on the uncomfortable work of antiracism, including taking reparative actions for black employees, such as addressing racial pay gaps and making commitments to advancement and succession planning that include people of color. Meaningful policy changes can level the playing field for highly qualified people of color and other underrepresented employees. Unearthing and eliminating conscious and unconscious biases goes a long way toward opening the gateway for significant change. DEI won't look like a marketing campaign but rather will feel like a relationship-building exercise. Instead of becoming transactional, it will be transformational. This will foster more natural friendships within the workplace and encourage the community to speak up about what they need.

Serious and honest DEI work may very well make corporate managers nervous, and that's okay. (Believe me, my company, The Lazu Group, hears it all the time.) Directly and indirectly, these business leaders voice the fear that they will lose their power as other communities make gains. Why wouldn't they feel this way? When the system is rigged in their favor and it barely feels like privilege, it's hard not to feel as though you're giving something up. It's a point I raise here and elsewhere in this book because it deserves emphasis: so much of the failure of early DEI work was because it underestimated the scarcity mentality that plagues so many people. Theirs is the untrue belief that if others win, they will lose.

That's why one of the big pieces of advice for corporate leaders is to understand and anticipate the reactions to the work. DEI work challenges an individual narrative of where they sit in society, a scary thing for most humans to do. When it comes to changing ingrained tradition, you need to expect and plan for the pushback that will naturally happen. Any leader working to incorporate DEI work needs to know how to navigate these waters and understand the ramifications for a company's culture. This will not be the last time you read this caution, because you cannot overstate it.

With DEI, change is inevitable, visible both inside and outside the organization. It looks like managers pausing to reconsider when they're about to say no to something that would help advance DEI. It looks like managers valuing people of color in the firm, regardless of hierarchy, and understanding the strategic value they bring. It looks like a culture that, for the first time, asks the deeper hiring questions: "Will we acknowledge that having another Harvard-educated white male does not add as much incremental value as hiring a black woman out of Howard University who has an MBA, or a woman of color from an immigrant family who understands how first-generation Americans view the marketplace and our products?"

What's great about DEI work is that it is not rocket science; it's actually elementary. Fairness, not bullying; giving people what they need to succeed—these are things we learned in school. Some people may actually be trying to teach their children these values right now.

This mission, and the purpose of this book, is to help demystify DEI conversations and provide tactics for how leaders can make effective change in themselves and in their companies and communities—how to move from intention to impact. Leaders, managers, and teams need to be better prepared for a future that is fluid, in color, and unafraid to demand visibility. Corporations that cannot show impact in DEI and across all categories of ESG are going to have trouble attracting and retaining talent and growing their customer base, and that will translate into struggling for relevance.

This book breaks down this new territory: how to navigate it and, most important, how to change to be successful. Part I explains how we got here and why this moment was inevitable. It includes a brief history of social movements from the political response to the gains of the civil rights movements of the sixties, the great crash of 2008 and its aftermath, and the movements of 2010 to the present, including Occupy Wall Street, Black Lives Matter, and March for Our Lives. These movements have led to real power shifts and have resulted in corporate boycotts and social shaming. Part I also discusses the work companies must do to actively fight racism while explaining that paying only lip service to DEI work without fully engaging can backfire.

Part II provides a blueprint for creating sustainable change in any company. It starts by understanding how a strong DEI culture is profitable and how firms can think about and set goals. After that, the next step is to uncover the cultural barriers to reaching those goals and then to develop strategies for overcoming those barriers, including decentralizing DEI work. Finally, companies need to find their authentic voice when engaging with outward-facing DEI work. Building greater connections outside the organization can help strengthen DEI efforts. One specific area is vendor procurement, another way for companies to diversify their networks.

Much of the content of this book is pragmatic. It provides a much-needed how-to framework for corporations to make meaningful contributions to the quest for racial justice, from engaging in true social inclusion to creating equal access to opportunity, regardless of race. But make no mistake: writing this book was an emotional journey for me. It was hard to find a balance between the work that needs to be done being seen as "success" and keeping the attempts that have been made in context. Knowing just how performative, new, and an uphill battle all this is, I include large businesses that are trying, but I want to be clear that none of these businesses would get a gold star from me for "achieving" DEI. To earn that gold star, a diverse community would have to tell the world that this company is a safe place to work and supports the community, and that it is proud to be associated with the company, whether as employees or as customers. Gold stars would also go to companies acknowledging their white privilege and maybe even creating budgets or incentive packages to establish more leadership positions to accommodate the promotion of talented people from diverse backgrounds and perspectives. Corporate America isn't there yet. Nonetheless, there are businesses that are in the process of trying and sometimes succeeding. These examples are works in progress, working through and despite white privilege.

Racial inequality is a persistent problem in America, but only because it is central to so much that history tells us to hold sacred. But the fact of the matter is, exclusion does not lead to sustainable growth—quite the opposite. By picking up this book you are a part of the solution, building new models for an America that understands the value of all of us growing an economy. What's needed now is your will to get started and evolve.

Let's get it right this time.

1 How We Got Here

Once embraced as drivers of economic growth and American exceptional-ism, corporations are now seen as perpetrators of injustice, from the racial wealth gap to climate change. Activist culture is triggering widespread questioning, and collective action is changing the way corporations and businesses are being held accountable in American society. In order to find the way forward, we need to understand how we got here.

1 Waking Up to Uncomfortable Truths

Years ago, while I was facilitating training for executives, we began talking about common microaggressions, such as making awkward comments about intelligence or characterizing oneself as "color-blind." Noticing that one of the executives had his head in his hands, I stopped and asked him if everything was all right. He looked up at me and said, "I have done a lot of what you have listed and am feeling stupid." We laughed and acknowledged how ignorant so many Americans are about the experience of people of color, but more specifically, how ignorant people reinforce their privilege. This is not by accident. Diversity, equity, and inclusion (DEI) work fails when it continues to define a problem rather than solve it. There is no single data set, training, or hire that will end bias. Seeing the evidence of racism or sexism is not enough to change behavior.

Corporate leadership is waking up to the truth that it can no longer afford to see equity work as simply a bonus or a "nice to have." Creating equity gets at the heart of how to sustain diversity and inclusion. Equity is *the quality of being fair*; in this context, equity means providing people with what they need to thrive. Corporations need to get equity right to remain competitive, and getting that right means shifting culture. It is now as essential to building a strong brand as being known for employee and consumer loyalty—especially following the Supreme Court affirmative action ruling.

Companies are finally beginning to understand that racial injustice is systemic and must be addressed holistically. The ultimate goal of any DEI work is to repair the outcomes of generational exclusion in business. Is there progress to point to? Yes, there are examples of companies that are genuinely trying and making some progress. But the examples are few and far between. Much more common are the stories of struggles and of trying to bridge the divides that come with systemic racism.

Unfortunately, for too many years, DEI efforts were framed as charity rather than as a real value-adding strategy. Moreover, diversity and inclusion efforts usually focused on hiring and were siloed into Human Resources departments. Hiring alone, however, does not create inclusion or equity. DEI work must also extend to professional development and promotion, to who has access to the leadership ranks, as well as to customers and overall company culture.

Once seen as catalysts of economic growth and American exceptionalism, corporations are now seen as perpetrators of injustice, driving everything from the racial wealth gap to climate change. What is the engine behind these changes? The activist culture is causing us to question and push these systems. Collective action is changing the way corporations and businesses are being held accountable in American society. Around the world, youth strikes demand urgent action against climate change. In the United States, movements such as Occupy Wall Street and Black Lives Matter are making waves and catalyzing change. There is no denying that more people are motivated to hold corporations accountable through direct action. It has changed how Americans see corporations' role in equity work and their own role as consumers.

Building a thriving and inclusive economy is within reach. Corporations are uniquely positioned through their size and infrastructure to make potentially global changes toward equity. By aligning social change with business priorities, corporations can build a new way to maintain profitability, one that leverages the benefits of inclusion as a response to the changing consumer and employee landscape.

The problem, however, is that most people in corporate America have no clue how to effectively respond to the moment in a way that is authentic and sustainable. It is hard to play catch-up in public, as many companies are finding out, but it does not have to be that way. That's why this book addresses not just thinking but also the practical strategies and tactics needed to support business leaders who want to guide their companies into the future. They are actively looking for ways to evolve their culture into one that embraces the business case for diversity and creates a feeling of belonging for all.

The Seven Stages from Intention to Impact

In my work with corporate clients, I witness and guide their journey as they move from intention to impact. The journey typically goes through seven stages, as I explain here and refer to throughout the book.

Stage 1: Feeling Excited Relief—There Is a Way to Solve "the Problem"

Everyone gets excited. Pledges are made, committees are formed. CEO action supporting DEI is a great first step.

- Far too many companies stop here, in this initial stage. When that happens, DEI campaigns can devolve into lip service that elicits eye rolls or are perceived as tone-deaf, causing the company to backpedal. To avoid doing more harm than good, companies need to stay the course and push on beyond stage 1 into the harder, deeper DEI work of the upcoming stages and maybe even backpedal from launching a tone-deaf DEI campaign.

Stage 2: Learning about "the Problem"

Most companies set up training sessions, book clubs, and education portals. Creating strategy and enabling employee resource groups (ERGs) are great ways to apply learning.

- A good way to go deeper (as our clients do) is actively working through what we call the "3 L's"—listening, learning, and taking loving action.

Stage 3: Taking Action on Low-Hanging Fruit

After training and learning, it's time to take some action. Most organizations start with the obvious and easy. For example, they include questions on equity in an employee survey, talk about DEI in group meetings and companywide town halls, and begin reviewing job descriptions for bias.

- At this stage, specific actions and outcomes include increased communication, diversity hiring commitments, and efforts to establish baselines and measure progress. Qualitative metrics are really important here; feelings and stories are data.

Stage 4: Denying There Is Pushback

Sometimes the initial small actions taken thus far are met with pushback. The communications team may start to push back about messaging.

Managers and team members ask whether the new policies will mean hiring "less-qualified" people or put the company at legal risk by centering BIPOC (Black, Indigenous, and people of color). While this pushback may feel valid, many times it is based in tradition.

- Those leading DEI efforts may often try to compromise at this point, which will dilute their efforts. They don't fully realize that the ingrained structures are pushing back—or, as philosopher and author Charles Mills puts it, ignorance is fighting back.[1]

Stage 5: Realizing the Pushback Is Real

Much of the pushback encountered can be explained by employees being afraid to take risks, worried they might get in trouble, or, worse yet, concerned they may be rejected by their work "tribe." The result is CYA culture (which we discuss more in chapter 7). "Covering your ass" behaviors show up in subtle (and sometimes not so subtle) questions or concerns. Many managers instinctively acquiesce to "concerns" expressed about DEI efforts until they realize that it's actually the machine pushing back. Executives who normally do not encounter resistance to their decisions suddenly have subordinates questioning their directives and making excuses.

- The key here is to recognize these reactions for what they are: pervasive bias. See that the problem isn't what's being requested; the problem is that this is about dismantling bias. For DEI teams, it is especially hard when the one who is pushing back is a person of color. As author and anthropologist Zora Neale Hurston said, "All my skinfolk ain't kinfolk."[2] For some, the safest way to survive is to join the power structure and repeat the narrative. It's important to have a third party to help maintain quality control for intention and actions.

Stage 6: Realizing the Pushback Is Bias

"I've worked with these guys for years, and they have never asked me the questions they asked about the minority-owned business I was suggesting we work with." This comment came from a white executive who was helping a minority-owned business enterprise (MBE) increase its clientele. He believed in the MBE and reached out to close friends he did business with, asking them to meet with this business. As he listened to their pushback he wondered why, since they didn't normally question introductions to potential business contacts, yet here they did.

- The realization that their pushback was bias really hurt his feelings and reinforced for him how even friendships are not immune. The pain of this realization often keeps people in denial.

Stage 7: Deciding to Move around and through the Bias

"Write the damn checks," advises investor Barbara Clarke,[3] who has been a champion angel investor with woman- and minority-owned business enterprises (WMBEs) for years. It's how she responds to white or male hesitancy in response to a pitch. She refuses to entertain questions asked about WMBEs that male investors did not pose to male entrepreneurs. In the same way, deciding to move through bias is the only way to put it behind you.

- Taking this step successfully means you don't have to go back to step 1. Ask yourself: Are you committed to the struggle or will you back down to the structural bias that wants to protect itself at all costs and slow down progress? Do you prefer being comfortable now if it affects future profitability, sustainability, and reputation?

By successfully navigating all seven stages, your company will be able to steer through the ongoing work DEI success requires. Soon the inclusive behavior becomes natural as the culture changes.

Diversity and Inclusion: The Power of Decentralization

Change in companies most commonly happens from the top down. Within a centralized structure, senior management identifies the desired change, along with the goals to be attained and the key performance indicators. Through incentives and admonishments (the proverbial carrots and sticks), leaders try to push people toward the attitudes, behaviors, decisions, and actions that will lead to the desired change.

The fact is, workplace culture is shaped by hierarchy. Regardless of how much CEOs and other senior leaders talk about having an open-door policy, most businesses are centralized structures. Companies love centralizing things out of the belief that it creates efficiencies and promotes accountability. But in matters of culture, centralization can feel authoritarian. With DEI in particular, a centralized approach rarely works. While support for DEI must absolutely come from the top, it cannot be forced through the system. The reason is simple: the politicization of race makes DEI an emotional trigger issue for many people. Add to that the dynamic of trying to push change, and people will feel as if management is encroaching on their personal values. It can also trigger exclusion fatigue among employees of color.

However, in decentralized infrastructures, everyone can be a leader. When it comes to DEI, this is of crucial importance. In my work with clients, from one of the largest financial services firms in the world to thought leaders on the front lines of social change, I can attest to the importance of decentralizing DEI. By decentralizing it, change happens at the human level, where people relate to each other. This also takes the burden off the Human Resources department, which must navigate a complex world of talent acquisition processes and policies, career development and promotions, and employment regulations. Moreover, HR is typically underfunded, overworked, and underappreciated. Changing culture from within a regulatory posture and hampered by insufficient resources is almost impossible.

Decentralizing DEI means putting more training, tools, resources, and empowerment where they are needed most: among middle managers, who are on the front lines of deciding who is hired, developed, and promoted. As research has found, middle managers are key to colleagues' experiences of belonging and feeling included.[4]

In "discovery groups" with employees at several firms, for example, I have heard from white managers who expressed a genuine desire to hire more diverse talent to bring new experiences and perspectives to their teams but did not know how to go about doing so within the strictures of talent acquisition policies. I've also heard the opposite: white managers who voiced skepticism about the value of DEI and committed microaggressions against employees of color, who repeatedly expressed feeling invisible, overlooked, and expected to "act white" in order to fit in.

As much as company leaders may say they want to foster an inclusive culture and champion genuine equity, my work with companies has shown that bottlenecks frequently occur at the middle manager level. That fact alone should convince companies of the value of decentralizing DEI. Because here's what is also true: when managers express a genuine desire to put DEI into action, they will reduce turnover and generate more profits. Then other managers will have to catch up or else be left behind.

As I discuss in upcoming chapters (see part II), decentralizing DEI starts with a shift in power at the C-suite and management committee levels. Middle managers who previously received (but often resisted) top-down dictates suddenly have front-line responsibility for DEI goals. The more DEI gets decentralized, the more people feel the shift and flow of power (and empowerment) throughout the organization. Bosses become peers, willing to learn from others. Rationality is replaced with emotional intelligence. A command-and-control structure gives way to empower-and-trust. The result is nothing less than transformation—a chance to make history.

Against the Grain

Much of my corporate work revolves around financial services and real estate development. For me, this is boots-on-the-ground work in some of the most economically influential industries and sectors that touch everyone—consumers, small-business owners, large companies, neighborhoods, cities. These industries are also largely dominated by white men, which makes DEI work challenging but also rewarding as we make headway. In addition, along the way I have encountered people, trailblazers and groundbreakers, who have gone against the grain of the dominant business culture. When examining their stories, we catch a glimpse of what equity—in terms of equal access and opportunity for all—can look like. As these development projects illustrate, the companies we work with have the power to make comprehensive change.

Philip Payton was one of the grandfathers of black real estate development. Working in Harlem, he helped build a working- and middle-class community in segregated New York City in the early 1900s. Payton attributed his first success to a dispute between two white landlords. One of the landlords asked Payton to fill his apartment with "Negroes" as revenge. After successfully filling the apartment, he started his life in development. Over the years, though, he has become a forgotten voice in equitable real estate development for an emerging middle class, which had once earned him the sobriquet "father of Black Harlem." Today, when I look at Payton, I see a trailblazer, an activist, and a business genius. His example is a reminder to business leaders everywhere that systemic change can and should happen in the context of doing business—productively, profitably, and profoundly.

Systems, Not Symptoms

Problems need to be solved at the system level, not the symptom level. It calls to mind an organizing parable I heard back in my twenties. It goes like this: one day you see a dead fish floating down the river. You think nothing of it, then you see ten dead fish, twenty, and a hundred. Suddenly it's very clear that there is something wrong. But the problem doesn't appear to be happening where you're standing on the riverbank. You need to go upstream and see who is poisoning the water and killing those fish.

This is as true with DEI work today as it was in social organizing decades ago because at the end of the day, somebody is always tampering with the river.

Corporate America needs its own "dead fish in the river" moment to stop fixating on symptoms and focus instead on the systemic causes of racism and inequality. But that's where the metaphor ends. DEI is not about rescuing, it's not an act of charity. American business is finally waking up to the fact that diversity is actually good for business and will grow our economy.

"We do believe, and we didn't just start believing, that [DEI] is both a business imperative and it's a core value," Robert Matthews, vice president and chief diversity, equity and inclusion officer at Exelon, an Illinois-based utility and energy company, told me in a roundtable discussion at MIT Sloan School of Management.[5] "We believe we can develop more bespoke solutions for our customers and community—we can do that better . . . and more effectively when we represent the community and the customers that we serve."

As businesses work to become more equitable, enterprises and industries will become stronger and more stable. This should come as no surprise; making money is such a huge part of American culture. As younger generations increasingly call for an equal society, corporate America has a moment to lead the way in this evolution. I heard these voices back in my work with Belafonte: *We're talented. We can do the work. We want a chance.* And I hear them now. DEI not only levels the playing field, it also expands it, increasing opportunity and wealth creation for all.

2 Evolve or Die

Evolution is one of the half-dozen shattering ideas that science has developed
to overturn past hopes and assumptions, and to enlighten our current thoughts.
—Stephen Jay Gould

White privilege and white supremacy are as fundamental to America as the
proverbial "life, liberty and pursuit of happiness," which from the beginning applied solely to white men. Even our emancipation hero, Abraham
Lincoln, did not center equity in ending slavery: "I will say then that I am
not, nor ever have been in favor of bringing about in any way the social and
political equality of the white and black races."[1] As the philosopher Charles
Mills states, "This historical reality is completely obfuscated in the myth of
an all-inclusive contract. . . . Far from being neutral the law and the state
were part of the racial polity apparatus of subordination, codifying whiteness as enforcing racial privilege."[2] This sobering truth is as self-evident
today as it was in colonial America and during the founding of the United
States. Because whiteness was a part of this country's creation, any solution
that ignores how important white privilege is would be disingenuous. And
this truth is why diversity, equity, and inclusion (DEI) work must start with
race, and with deconstructing white privilege. To do otherwise is to enter
DEI work in denial of how black became the opposite of white, and how
blackness therefore establishes whiteness.

Mills also reminds us of the actual journey to equity when he writes,
"So though progress has obviously been made in comparison to the past,
the appropriate benchmark should not be the very low bar of emancipation from slavery and the formal repeal of Jim Crow but the simple idea

of racial equality."[3] Or as Chris Rock says, "Stop looking for credit for s**t you're supposed to do." Therefore, to see impact in DEI work, we have to dismantle the systems that reinforce the unearned privilege associated with being white.[4]

America received a shocking wake-up call about the state of racism on May 25, 2020, when cops in Minneapolis added another martyr to the movement against police brutality specifically and the movement for civil rights in general. George Floyd was brutally and callously murdered by four police officers who responded to a call about someone suspected of using a counterfeit twenty-dollar bill. Before we jump into the effect Floyd's murder had on society, we need to take a moment to consider just how traumatized and terrorized the black community already felt. That was as true on May 24, 2020, as it was during the civil rights movement. Despite all the dreams and promises, the hard work and martyrdom, very little has changed in America.

Policing in America has its roots in slave patrols, an activity that policed black bodies to reinforce structural subjugation. Such patrols were about maintaining order, not about crime prevention, as Connie Hassett-Walker, a researcher in racial, ethnic, and gender disparities in the criminal justice system and an associate professor of criminal justice at Norwich University, writes.[5] The Jim Crow era was a time in America after emancipation that worked to resubjugate a newly freed black community. *Plessy v. Ferguson,* the court case that reaffirmed the separate but equal doctrine, is one legal precedent that highlights the continued structural subjugation.

In a racially segregated America, lynching serves a brutally effective purpose: keeping order and putting people in their place through violence. We have all seen the pictures of the white community seeming to enjoy a day at the park, in their Sunday best. It may take a second to realize the motivation for their convening: a black body hanging from a tree. Lynching a black person reinforces the power and privilege of whiteness and sends a clear message to the black community to submit to the will of any white person. Lynchings were a common tactic used after the Civil War to stop newly freed slaves from ever feeling free. According to the Tuskegee Archives, considered the most comprehensive totaling up of lynchings reported, 4,743 lynchings occurred between 1881 and 1968; the vast majority, 3,446 were of African Americans.[6] Even in the twentieth century, law enforcement turned a blind eye to these acts of domestic terrorism, and sometimes officers of the law were even participants, such as in 1936, when Atlanta police officer Samuel Roper and another police officer knocked on the door of the Finch family at midnight and asked for Tom Finch Jr. An hour later he was left for dead in front of the hospital where he worked as an orderly. His face was beaten to a pulp, and he had been shot multiple times. He died on the operating table. His last words were "Oh, Lord."[7]

And so George Floyd became the latest in a string of lynchings, which also included Ahmaud Arbery, who was chased by two white men (one a sheriff) and shot in the street, and Breonna Taylor, shot dead in her apartment after being awakened by plainclothes detectives in the middle of the night claiming to be searching for drugs. These murders were met with protests both locally and nationally, and many Americans attempted to hold police accountable. While many of these protests got mixed reactions from the white community, Floyd's murder changed all of that—a widely shared video and, later, body camera footage that captured every agonizing second of the nine minutes and twenty-nine seconds that police officer Derek Chauvin knelt on Floyd's neck, suffocating him. Then there was the lack of a government response, the egregious behavior of then president Donald Trump and his thinly veiled attempts to appease his white supremacist followers. After multiple failed attempts at making a statement about Floyd's murder, Trump's most decisive action was to authorize teargassing of peaceful protesters to clear the path for his photo op at a church (much to the anger of church leaders). This came just days after Trump declared himself "your president of law and order" and demanded that governors use the National Guard to "dominate the streets."[8]

In the absence of both presidential leadership and reason at this flashpoint, former president Barack Obama took a highly visible stance. "This is not an either-or. This is a both-and to bring about real change," he said. "We both have to highlight a problem and make people in power uncomfortable, but we also have to translate that into practical solutions and laws that could be implemented and monitored and make sure we're following up on."[9]

Business leaders, meanwhile, also responded with the best of intentions and all the grace of a cat on roller skates. They were shocked at the video capturing Floyd's murder. Once again, the streets were on fire. Their shock and disbelief—*How could this happen?*—was evidence of just how out of touch corporate America was with the reality of the racial reckoning being felt by

Americans, including their own employees. This shock reflects what Mills calls white ignorance—and the observations that white ignorance seems to fight against and does not want to resolve itself. As Mills writes, "The white delusion of racial superiority insulates itself against refutation."[10] In other words, white people are acculturated to ignore daily ongoing oppressions needed to create a privileged class, so that when something atrocious happens, America (dominated by white culture) responds with shock, seeing it as unbelievable. For the BIPOC community, however, it is very believable and all too common.

The $16 Trillion Loss

Corporate America appears to be slowly hearing the message that diversity is good for business, and most companies have DEI missions and goals. But how many companies really understand the size of their past loss—and their potential for future gain? In a 2020 report, Citibank estimated that if four key gaps experienced by blacks—in wages, education, housing, and investment—had been closed twenty years earlier, the U.S. economy would have reaped more than $16 trillion over that time. If those same gaps were closed now, the U.S. GDP would see a $5 trillion increase over the next five years.[11] The numbers are undeniably huge, and the source of this analysis as undeniably Wall Street as it gets—Citibank.

Diverse teams outperform nondiverse teams; there is no question that this is true. As McKinsey states in its 2020 *Diversity Wins* report, "I&D [inclusion and diversity] is a powerful enabler of business performance. . . . In short, diversity wins, now more than ever."[12] I've seen this countless times in my work. What's really interesting is that most CEOs with whom I work do not necessarily consider themselves progressive. A lot of them supported Ronald Reagan as president, and they believe deeply in capitalism as the engine to generate good in society (along with profits). Despite this thinking, they come to me because they also understand that within their markets there are swaths of communities not being served. Untapped growth potential does not sit in white America; rather, it is in diverse markets. They know they are missing out on opportunities to sell more goods and services to people who can become good customers. For example, from Rockland Trust to Eastern Bank, the CEOs of Boston financial institutions have been pushing more banking services for women- and minority-owned business enterprises (WMBEs). The more these CEOs I work with learn, the more they become powerful allies for black and brown communities—residents and business owners alike. Their motivation goes beyond philanthropy and social good works. They want to make more money.

So if making more is a driving force in business, and if we are not going to question capitalism (which I am more than willing to do, but for now let's go with it), then it's time to get real. There *is* more money to be made by being inclusive. Greater innovation comes from being diverse. It should NOT be hard for reasonable capitalists to move toward diversity and to create new markets where the racism blind spot has limited their potential. Therefore, any company that allows racism to hold it back is letting competitors take the lead. The best way to make money these days is from ideas—the diversity of thinking and fresh perspectives that result from becoming more inclusive of women and people of color.

Unfortunately, though, racism remains entrenched in American society and in corporate America. That's what holds us all back, so we need to actively fight racism in order to open up more opportunities for everyone. Becoming inclusive will make us more money together—the pie grows, for you and for me.

Corporate White Privilege

Virtually every organization says it is dedicated to DEI and belonging, and all businesses claim to want to attract the best talent. Yet most businesses lack diversity, especially at the top, where performance can make or break the entire company. The belief that only white men have good ideas is preposterous, and yet the composition of just about any C-suite would suggest that. Since the establishment of the Fortune 500 in 1955, only nineteen black CEOs have led those companies out of a total of 1,800 top executives.[13] In 2022, only six of the Fortune 500 companies had a black CEO.[14] Even our leadership archetypes are white males, as Brandy Mabra, a black woman and CEO, wrote in a 2022 article for *Fast Company*. In it, she describes her excitement of writing her first article for a national business publication until she saw the stock image selected by the publication to represent "a leader"—a white man standing in front of a group of colleagues.[15] As an entrepreneur, business consultant, CEO, and a woman of color I can certainly relate. What's wrong with this picture, indeed!

White privilege in a company goes a long way toward explaining why most companies cannot move the needle to respond to the demands for greater diversity from consumers and employees alike; as a result, they then fail to see the positive impacts of DEI at their company. An intention to diversify does not alone create the impact. Impact comes from bringing the intention to life in a company and shifting the culture to place greater value on diversity, not just because it's the right thing to do but because it's smart business.

Any business leader knows that no matter how successful they are today, the future is not guaranteed. Not being able to read the proverbial tea leaves and innovate accordingly can quickly cause their organization to lose its competitive edge, market share, and brand reputation. The classic examples include Kodak failing to recognize digital photography, Blockbuster not seeing Netflix coming, and MySpace being unable to compete with Facebook. All are examples of once industry-leading firms that failed to evolve in a changing world. We face the same inflection point today. The twenty-first century is innovating socially, and companies that are not reading it right will struggle to remain competitive. The solution is confronting and disrupting racism.

As an organizer, I have made combating America's racism part of my work for over twenty years. I have known America is racist, I have learned and seen the violent outcomes of history bearing down on the present; yet over these past few years I have needed to catch my breath at the pace of violence. The 2020s have already become one of the most devastating decades in recent history. Growing inequity, racial tension, and failing infrastructure have all led to our inability to respond to COVID-19 as a cohesive society. The pandemic laid bare all our vulnerabilities and became a crucible for the racial violence that has always been bubbling just beneath the surface. The compounding effect of neglect has fed our inability to effectively address the crisis. Fortunately, ongoing activism—and with new generations joining—has created a tipping point for systems change, and not a moment too soon.

In an AP-NORC poll, one-third of respondents (U.S.-born adults) said they believed they were being replaced by immigrants.[16] That's a high number, but it does not account for the whole story. Among the poll respondents, two-thirds did not hold this belief. It is a reason for some guarded optimism and where, ultimately, we will find the solution. Corporate

America must play a significant role in leveraging any openness to finally address racism and end white privilege.

An Investment in Equity

Currently, millennials are the most diverse generation. By 2040 white people will be a minority population (while continuing to hold most of the wealth).[17] The most educated demographic in America currently is black women, who have been obtaining degrees at a consistently high rate for nearly a decade.[18] And yet CEOs opine on how hard it is to find diverse talent. These conflicting statistics and overall changes to the status quo have caused everyday Americans to question the longevity and even inevitability of such structures as Wall Street and corporate America. The moral dilemma over racism has catapulted activism into a core value for many Americans. As a consumer culture, we vote with our wallets; the result is a resounding 87 percent of the population reporting the desire for the brands they purchase to do good in the world.[19] This emerging bottom line is rapidly becoming as important as a secret sauce or brand logo.

Corporate executives are leading their companies through a generational shift from the boomers to today's millennials and Gen-Zers. Today's youth are activist generations with different expectations of both their chosen products and their employers. In many ways the children of executives probably understand the cultural ramifications of this change better than most of the C-suite leaders. Mindful corporations have been dedicating resources to find methods to evolve their culture and curate offerings to appear more attractive to an increasingly diverse America. However, simply allocating money without first establishing a deeper understanding of the history and issues and then creating a long-lasting, adoptable, and adaptable strategy will ultimately result in failure to fix the problem. Close to $50 billion has been committed to fight bias since May 2020[20] without a true understanding of how best to leverage that money toward sustainable impact. The fix will take informed money and sustained action. And with $16 trillion lost because of bias, as tallied by Citibank, it is worth the investment.

CEOs and management are being confronted by new challenges and opportunities as they navigate a future for their companies. Companies are facing existential pain points such as climate change, pandemic recovery, and racial repair. These are uncharted waters for most executives as tensions rise between short- and long-term thinking. Shareholders expect results, employees want to feel they are part of a socially responsible company, and customers want to reward companies that do the right thing with long-term loyalty. The stakes are too high for companies not to get it right.

Disney is a great example of a company that struggled to please everyone as it navigated the culture wars.[21] The company found itself in hot water for many reasons, from its history of racist cartoons to its lack of diverse princesses on its fairytale roster. As Florida continued to slide into reactionary laws, such as the "don't say gay" law, Disney found itself once again in the headlines for donating to homophobic elected officials in Florida while simultaneously courting the LGBTQIA+ community through efforts like Gay Day in the parks. The callout from the LGBTQIA+ community was swift and strong. Hundreds of Disney employees also walked off the job in protest.[22] In response, Disney tried to send a donation to Human Rights Campaign (HRC), a national gay advocacy organization, which refused the donation until it saw meaningful action to stop the hateful law. Disney continued the dance, making commitments to hire and increase representation in its movies and other content. Then-CEO Bob Chapek met with HRC leadership to deliver his mea culpa in person. A Disney heir came out as transgender at the HRC national gala, while the current generation has continued to distance itself from the company created by its grandfathers by donating a $250,000 matching challenge to support HRC efforts. This is the stuff of headlines and a never-ending stream of editorials. For business leaders, it is a cautionary tale of what not to do. As Chapek found out, trying to appease both sides made him weak and cost him his job. Disney replaced him Bob Iger, who came out of retirement to lead the company and face the mounting political fight in Florida.

Capitalism is a philosophy, and like all good philosophies it evolves with the times. Founding economic thought leaders such as Adam Smith and John Stuart Mill were aiming to define a new way forward based on individual rights, private ownership, and industrialism. The hypocrisy and weakness in this philosophy are exposed by the growth of capitalism based on stealing land and owning individuals. Even Adam Smith saw the power dynamics when he observed, "The persons who make all the laws in that country are persons who have slaves themselves. These will never make any laws mitigating their usage; whatever laws are made with regard to slaves are intended to strengthen the authority of the masters and reduce the slaves to a more absolute subjection."[23] It is in this hypocrisy that we see our evolution with the idea that capitalism can be more than extractive.

The challenge, however, is that corporate leaders may not know how to change or respond to these new expectations. Do they know the communities and problems well enough to innovate impactful solutions? Do they know how to step aside and let those closest to the problem create the solution? Can they identify the true fix? Is their ultimate goal equality or equity? Are they hoping to diversify their networks or achieve specific hiring goals? Admittedly, it can all feel very overwhelming.

The result of facing such complex and emotionally charged issues causes many executives to both unconsciously and consciously slow these efforts, stifling culture shifts and social change. In addition to the fear of getting it catastrophically wrong, there is a gap between intention and impact into which many executives have fallen. It's no surprise that their DEI efforts have become largely a series of check boxes forced on middle managers, while excluded communities are blamed for the efforts not working.

Corporations have achieved amazing things when they have put their mind to it, from creating vaccines to creating a commercial space industry. Yet the numbers on DEI are consistently abysmal. According to McKinsey, black employees made up 14 percent of the employees at companies participating in its analysis. At the managerial level, however, black representation dropped to 7 percent, and at the higher level of senior manager, vice president, and senior vice president, it was only 4–5 percent.[24] These numbers attest to a bitter truth: corporate America is determined to find a way to change without exactly changing its structure.

How We Got Here: 1980 Social Justice Clawbacks

To understand how to respond to this moment, we first must understand how we got here. While the narrative starts centuries ago when all those European philosophers were figuring out how to be free, we will focus on recent American history to see the cycles that push the country toward justice. The 1980s is the decade in which most millennials were born and the era that shaped their childhoods. The country was healing from the civil rights movement wins and murders, a presidential resignation, and an oil crisis. Affirmative action and other results of the civil rights movement were being scrutinized as overreaching and unsustainable. White society was ready to claw back the gains made by people of color generally and black people in particular.

Taking the race playbook from Barry Goldwater's presidential run in 1964, Ronald Reagan entered national politics with a Republican National Committee (RNC) slogan that might sound familiar: Let's Make America Great Again. The RNC used the fear of losing a white, male-dominated society as a campaign message, putting gains for minorities in the crosshairs. Reagan's legacy became one of civil rights rollbacks, draconian drug laws featuring mandatory minimum sentences, and a widening of the wealth gap. The policies of Reagan actively dismantled the legislative wins of the civil rights movement and took actions such as supporting seniority over diversity goals, waging a racist war on drugs, and creating the welfare queen narrative, which dehumanized working-class black women.

The Reagan administration professed what it called a "color-blind" approach to civil rights, to preserve the rights of blacks and whites. This position justifiably drew the ire of Benjamin L. Hooks, NAACP executive director, and Vernon Jordan, former president of the National Urban League, who stood firm on the need for affirmative action to redress bias against blacks and women. An article published in the *New York Times* quoted Hooks's remarks in a TV interview: "The Reagan Administration acts as if the white male is the minority."[25] In the Reagan administration's first case taking on affirmative action, it coined the term "reverse discrimination." On April 2, 1985, Reagan's Justice Department filed to overturn affirmative action plans in fifty-six counties, cities, and states. This radical action by the president was a clear message that the country no longer prioritized the goals of the civil rights movement.

Reagan's attacks on affirmative action represented only one theater in the war against black people. His war on drugs had much sharper teeth and put the police at the center of black society. If you are of a certain age, "Just Say No" was a part of your fifth-grade education and lexicon. The program explained that drugs were bad, and their sellers and users deserved harsh punishment. I remember in my DARE class police officers asked whether anyone's parents did drugs, encouraging kids to share anything they may have seen. I look back now and realize this was more than drug education; it was policing through education.

The war on drugs was actually a war on black people and urban centers throughout the country, and it used draconian policies, such as mandatory prison time for nonviolent drug offenses. Make no mistake: this was a policy targeted to jailing black people. For example, five grams of crack (80 percent of crack users were black) would get you five years in prison. You would need to get caught with 500 grams of cocaine (a drug primarily used by white people, and the same one that is used to make crack) to get the same time.[26] Not only did this "war" send hundreds of thousands of black people to jail for years for nonviolent offenses, it signaled an open season for police to take control of black and brown neighborhoods through excessive force. This did not end with Reagan. Presidents George Bush and Bill Clinton continued Reagan-era antidrug policies, with Clinton increasing the antidrug budget by 25 percent.[27]

As the war on drugs gives way to the legalization of cannabis, how many of those businesses are run by black and brown entrepreneurs whose communities were most affected by those draconian laws? Are the prisoners who were convicted of weed crimes, which are no longer offenses with state legalization and the introduction of big business in this space, now free? This has yet to be equitable.

From Reagan to Occupy Wall Street

If the Reagan administration was the end of the New Deal era, then the 2008 financial crisis marked the beginning of the end of over-romanticizing Reaganomics and scapegoating people of color. Americans were ready for a real conversation around what's next. Yet what came next was disappointing for Main Street: when Wall Street got bailed out, America found out some banks were "too big to fail," even as families lost homes and retirement savings.

Over the next few years, while President Barack Obama and his team worked to get the American economy back on track (and get Americans health care), many entering the workforce were unable to find jobs. The recovery was slow, and slowest for those with the least.

From 2007 to 2009 the poverty rate grew to 15 percent[28] and millions of Americans suffered financial insecurity. In 2010 the wealth of the median household headed by a person born in the 1980s was nearly 25 percent below what earlier generations in the same age group had accumulated. Millennials became known as the lost generation for their loss of wealth and lack of economic growth.

Cut to the summer of 2010. It was a busy one for direct action organizers. Tired of watching Wall Street recover at the expense of Main Street, anticonsumerism organizations were about to launch a movement that would change how we talk about class in America. Around this time, op-eds describing the growing class divide were appearing in the mainstream press, including from such authors as Warren Buffett and Robert Reich. Warren Buffett did not mince words in his *New York Times* article titled "Stop Coddling the Super-Rich." He urged the government to tax the rich, saying it would not hurt investment.[29] Buffett tapped into how tired the average American was of a recovery that did not include the working and middle classes. The growing tension culminated on September 17, 2011, when over one thousand people joined the call to march to the opening bell of the stock exchange after gathering in Zuccotti Park, and continued to occupy the park for two months. In a few weeks, the world would see this tactic used around the globe to call attention to wealth inequality.

Millions of people globally occupied their economic centers, including hundreds of thousands in cities around the United States. Occupy Wall Street reinvigorated direct action and a class conversation for the fed-up 99 percent. Unions, social justice organizers, and class activists joined forces again to reignite consumer activism. Occupy, whose story is often told as one of failure, actually marks a new dawn of tactical organizing that would be a catalyzing force toward evolving capitalism in the twenty-first century. As author Jon Meacham wrote in *Time* magazine, "The Occupy Wall Street protests at last suggest that America's wealth gap is once again becoming an organizing political principle in the country."[30]

Did it work? Consider that both Elizabeth Warren and Bernie Sanders have Occupy Wall Street DNA baked into their meteoric rise to national political prominence. "The top 1 percent" is now common in the lexicon. Closing the wealth gap is a focus of billions of dollars in philanthropy, and the Green New Deal was created as a policy outcome over the concerns raised by Occupy Wall Street. A movement against systemic oppression was ready to break new ground. Police killing black people is nothing new, but more people were paying attention and becoming outraged. Three young black women, Alicia Garza, Opal Tometi, and Patrisse Cullors, started a hashtag on Twitter that would go on to become the rallying cry for an end to the state-sanctioned police killing of black people. #BlackLivesMatter was a call for dignity in response to George Zimmerman claiming self-defense and subsequently being found not guilty in the 2012 shooting death of Trayvon Martin, a child holding Skittles. It continued to be used to express love for black life after Michael Brown was killed by a police officer and his body remained lying in the street, uncovered, for hours. The Ferguson, Missouri, response to Brown's death was seen globally, and the masses once again demanded accountability. At its height in July 2016, #BlackLivesMatter was being tweeted 500,000 times a day.[31]

This hashtag was more than a social media campaign; it was embedded in the new wave of the civil rights movement and was coming to life in the streets. Black Lives Matter (BLM) groups organized locally and nationally. They convened and created an agenda calling for the end of the war on black people, including criminal and economic justice reform through the BREATH Act. In 2016, Alton Sterling and Philando Castile were killed on July 5 and 6, respectively. BLM networks were ready: 112 protests in eighty-eight cities demanded accountability. With continued and sustained action against police killings, the movement for black lives can claim several victories locally and nationally, including electing local officials such as Jamaal Bowman as well as Congresswoman Cori Bush, who beat a corporate-backed Democrat to claim a seat in the House of Representatives. BLM continues to make inroads into mainstream America. According to a recent Pew poll, 67 percent of Americans support BLM goals.[32]

This fundamental passion for justice and expanded public attention included other successful movements, such as the Deferred Action for Childhood Arrivals (DACA) legislation and DREAMer movement, both of which shaped the immigration debate and national policy. The #MeToo movement led to a resurgence in women naming their experience of sexual harassment in the workplace and the world. This era also saw our youth marching for their lives, with high school students demanding #NeverAgain in response to gun violence in schools. The people had been set alight with the fire for justice.

Then in 2020, COVID-19 stopped us all in our tracks, literally. The virus destroyed much, but sadly not racism. Alongside the souls claimed by the pandemic, the inaction to stop oppression in our society claimed Floyd, Taylor, Aubrey, and so many more publicly lynched people. So even in the middle of a global pandemic, the movement could not and did not stop. The spirit of activism is alive and well, and corporate America will soon face greater accountability.

Where Are We Now? Boycotts and Reputational Risks

As we discuss throughout this book, the younger generations are a force for change, from protecting the environment to supporting BIPOC-owned businesses. At a time when the government seems to be too paralyzed to respond to the policy needs being sought by a majority of the country, corporations are being targeted to do something to evolve our current state and innovate change.

As we witnessed, 2021 was a bumper year for boycotts. In April, Georgia passed one of the most restrictive voting rights laws in the country in response to the overwhelming black participation in state and national elections in 2020 organized by Stacey Abrams and LaTosha Brown. New state laws restricted early voting, required voter IDs, and even prohibited giving out water to people waiting in line for hours to vote. Campaigns to boycott Georgia were swift, and a few days later more than one hundred CEOs joined a call to talk about how best to move forward. Major League Baseball pulled out of the All-Star Game and Home Depot became a target for corporate accountability campaigns that counted among their numbers pastors and clergy.

While the response is a start, all I kept thinking was, why did they wait until the law passed? Why not act proactively to apply pressure before people lost their voting rights? Did they not understand how this law would affect their ability to serve consumers, employees, and competitiveness? If these leaders had businesses in Georgia, were they thinking about their employees now living under Jim Crow 2.0? Why do businesses seem to wait until others sound calls of outrage—why not be on the leading edge of change?

Boycotts of companies for their failure to be equitable is becoming commonplace because of direct action. Direct action movements do more than bring people to the streets, they create momentum for more targeted action such as the boycott. The last ten years have seen a rise in justice organizations using boycotts to pressure corporations to change. As a call for the community to stop supporting companies that make wrong moves, boycotts are effective because they create a huge reputational risk. To be on the wrong side of history costs you today. Just look at MyPillow. The CEO's alliances with the far right and the resulting boycott cost the company $65 million in business.[33]

With activism on full display for the greatest part of most young people's lives, they have become sophisticated consumers and activists. With extraordinarily little government response following the Parkland, Florida, shooting at Marjory Stoneham Douglas High School, resulting in the deaths of seventeen people, teens came together to say enough is enough. They called for people to boycott companies that give money to the NRA. And their actions (along with movements such as Drain the NRA) were effective. Companies responded by pulling donations. And in 2020 the NRA filed for bankruptcy—down, but not out—a victory for the movement. And yet the NRA still went ahead with its convention, boycotted even by gun companies, days after the horrific Uvalde, Texas, shooting at Robb Elementary School.[34] Legislatively, some progress has finally been made, after decades of stonewalling by conservatives. In June 2022, President Biden signed a bipartisan gun law. Although the legislation did not go as far as Democrats had hoped, it did provide for expanded background checks for gun buyers under age twenty-one, with the intention of allowing more time for checks of juvenile and mental health records. The bill also provided funding for mental health and other intervention programs.[35]

Corporations have been spurred to action by consumer pressure, some of it as severe as boycotts and other as subtle as poor social media sentiment. They have made bold commitments to address all manner of social ills, including the extreme socioeconomic imbalance in the United States. Many of these commitments, however, are seated in charity and therefore have a limited and short-term impact and need to be repeated over and over without producing significant solutions to the underlying fundamental problems. For the next few generations, diversity, social responsibility, and overall progress will become more of deciding factors for consumers in terms of brand choice and loyalty. Consumers and employees alike are demanding that corporations not only act, but act to produce real system change.

America is not changing; it has changed. Consumers are holding corporations to a higher level of accountability as a result of the desire to innovate toward a more equitable culture. The question is, how well do corporations understand what is being asked of them in this moment of cultural shift?

The intense focus on American systems failures in the economic, health, and race crises have uncovered much about the systemic ills. These broken systems not only are costing us money, they are also dampening potential growth and overall profitability across the business landscape. Our current corporate culture is nonresponsive to new expectations, leaves money on the table, and denies America's corporations the best talent and ideas. This is surely motivation enough for any executive looking to ensure future financial viability.

"The times they are a-changin'," Bob Dylan sang in the '60s, and the current times are creating a demand for change in our societal structures. Therefore, for companies to remain relevant, systems must change. Innovation and cultural revision will lead to increased profitability if done right. There has never been a better time to evolve. Getting this moment right will not only substantially benefit the companies that get it right but could also help build a diverse middle class and keep America competitive globally. Younger generations are demanding a more just world and will reward those who help them get there. CEOs can be trailblazers instead of roadblocks to this new society.

3 Making Antiracism the New Normal

In a racist society, it's not good enough to be non-racist. We must be antiracist.
—Angela Davis

It was 2017, and I was part of a TV pilot that sought to bring together people in blue and red states. The project never launched, but I got a few powerful stories from the experience—for example, how I ended up in Alabama where Doug Jones, a Democrat, was running in a special election for the U.S. Senate seat vacated by Republican Jeff Sessions, who had resigned to become U.S. attorney general. Jones faced Roy Moore, a staunch Trump supporter and former Alabama State Supreme Court justice, who at the time was viewed as the frontrunner despite facing allegations of sexual assault and sexual misconduct against women, including some who allegedly were minors at the time. To say it was a politically charged time and place would be putting it mildly. I found myself, a progressive, talking to Trump supporters who backed Moore.

And then we went to C. J.'s home. Getting out of the car at his home, I was immediately greeted by a Confederate flag fluttering on a wall outside. I froze, unsure of whether I could make it all the way up the walk to his door. I was the only person of color in the group.

As we began talking, I straight up asked C. J., "What does that flag outside mean to you?"

"It's our history," he said, as if stating the obvious.

"Can you imagine what that flag represents for me?" I asked him.

"Oh, my family didn't own any slaves," he told me. "So that's not what it's about for me."

It was surreal. In the midst of a polite conversation, the most egregious argument was being made. C. J. kept protesting that he "didn't come from slave-owning whites," solely because his family had been poor—too poor to own slaves—as if that excused him from any racist connotation of displaying a Confederate flag outside his home.

At this point, I felt myself being triggered. I was shaking, but fought to remain in control of my emotions. Thankfully, I was with someone in our group who realized how traumatized I was and could validate my feelings, although to this day, he says he did not know how to respond while I was so emotionally paralyzed. That proved to be an important lesson for him as well.

After we left C. J.'s it took me a while to process what had happened, with C. J. claiming not to have a responsibility to the terror of the flag because his family had been too poor to own slaves. This echoed so much of the white rhetoric in society today. *It's not us. We're not racists. We didn't do that. We're not personally responsible.* . . . What they cannot see, however, is the effect of systemic racism in the United States for the past four hundred years—a system that has institutionalized white supremacy. Simply saying "I'm not racist" is not only egregious for the C. J.s of the world but also for corporate America, which continues to pay lip service—and only lip service—to changing the paradigms of who gets hired, promoted, and brought into positions of influence. Racism will continue until we have a groundswell of an antiracist movement of people who are willing to recognize their attitudes and behaviors that, consciously or unconsciously, are racist. The explicit truth here is we all participate in systems that perpetuate racism, and we all buy into racist beliefs. Therefore, "not being a racist" is not a moral stance; it's denial. As one of my friends who does white ally work says, "If you tell me, 'I'm not racist,' I will tell you that you are a liar. And if I tell you, 'I'm not racist,' you should tell me I'm a liar." This hard truth is where the work really begins.

The reason why racism has a stickiness in society, making it so difficult to shed, is because we don't actually know what the alternative is. One of the effective ways to change the paradigms and get rid of white ignorance is with antiracism. Ibram X. Kendi and other critical race theorists[1] have spoken about becoming antiracist, which is probably the best phrase to capture the opposite of racism for now. Justice would be my preferred word, but antiracism seems to be sticking, so I am happy to run with the term.

So how to be antiracist? What does antiracism look like? As Kendi states in his bestselling *How to Be an Antiracist*, "Racist ideas have defined our society since its beginning and can feel so natural and obvious as to be banal, but antiracist ideas remain difficult to comprehend, in part because they go against the flow of this country's history."[2] Antiracism looks like actively dismantling racism. To do that, we first need to know what it is so we can discern what it isn't.

The introductory training that my firm does with most of our business clients is called "Bias to Belonging." This training begins by explaining what bias is. Whenever we do this training, we see how many people don't understand the basics of racism and bias and what their antidotes are.

First, let's be clear here: there is no shortage of bias in this world. Here we are going to uncover and discuss what I call the "big three"—structural, institutional, and implicit biases. We can view these three biases as foundational to the American myth, cementing the hierarchy with straight white males at the top. That's why we need to attack the big three in order to have maximum impact.

Structural bias sits within large social systems and shared agreements for governance. "Structural" characterizes such practices and policies as slavery, the draft, inequality in public education, inequality in immigration, the war on drugs, redlining, and housing policy. This infection of racism is part of the DNA of American society. Structural bias informs and is reinforced by a second bias, institutional. These two biases are closely related because they have the most power. The distinction is in the nuances. For example, redlining and inequality in public education are structural because they are rooted in government policies; they become institutional because they are carried out in the biased and discriminatory actions of institutions and organizations—for example, banks and school districts. Such interconnectedness makes bias in the United States holistic and ubiquitous because it sits at all levels.

A great example of institutional bias is policies that prohibit natural hairstyles, such as afros, braids, bantu knots, and locs, which have been used to justify the removal of black children from school and black adults from work. As the NAACP Legal Defense Fund has observed, "Hair discrimination is rooted in systemic racism, and its purpose is to preserve white spaces."[3] To fight this form of institutional bias, organizers turned to a structural solution: the introduction of the CROWN Act of 2021—Creating a Respectful and Open World for Natural Hair. This law, being adopted state by state, seeks to protect people with natural black hair styles from being discriminated against. It prohibits institutions and employers from denying employment and educational opportunities because of hair texture or style.

The third bias is implicit or unconscious bias, and it dwells within the individual. This happens when you assume people's characteristics based on their outward appearance. Common forms include assuming people who do not speak English are not smart, all Asians are good at IT, or black people like football.

Often implicit biases are informed and shaped by structural and institutional biases, especially in the case of white supremacy, white ignorance, and viewing the world through a white lens. "Karens" are a great recent example of such trends, morphing from a meme for bossy women to representing white privilege and white supremacy in the kind of behavior that justifies in a woman's (usually) mind calling the cops on her neighbors of color.[4] (Men who engage is this behavior are sometimes called "Kens.") Consider what happened to Christian Cooper, an avid birdwatcher in Central Park, who merely asked a woman to keep her dog on a leash, as required by the park's regulations. She called 911 to say this black man was threatening her.[5]

The creation of white-only space provides a direct link between implicit and institutional biases and leads directly to structural bias, such as the criminal justice system. Until seventy-five years ago, black people did not have the same rights as whites. One way that whites maintained their control was through creating institutions where black people were not welcomed and setting double standards, one for white people and one for people of color.

Emmett Till was a black teenager in 1955 when a white woman accused him of whistling at her. The woman was Carolyn Bryant Donham, who at the time was married to Roy Bryant, one of the two men who were charged with abducting and brutally murdering Till. The two men were acquitted, but later confessed. In June 2022, nearly seventy years later, an unserved arrest warrant for Carolyn Bryant (her name at the time) was found in a box in a courthouse basement. This white woman was never made to stand accountable for her actions that led directly to Till's murder.[6] She died at the ripe old age of eighty-nine in April 2023, while Till had been only fourteen. It is an egregious example of implicit bias, grounded in the myth of the purity of white women and defended by deeply racist structural and institutional biases. When left unchallenged, these three biases have the power to enslave and murder others.

The antidote to this violent cycle of exclusion is working through what I like to call "the ladder to belonging." While "diversity, equity, and inclusion" provides the nomenclature for this work, it does not actually capture the North Star we define as "a place where people belong." Once we see diversity as a social fact, the question becomes, what do we do with that diversity? Inclusion is the next step, but it is not enough. Including people does not actually shift the culture to ensure that those who are intentionally being excluded actually feel they belong there. That's how BIPOC people feel in America: being included, but not really. Diversity and inclusion are an important start, but without equity they are incomplete. When diversity and inclusion are given cursory treatment, and people continue to be treated unfairly and inequitably, too often the blame falls on those who feel that they don't belong. Equity is the tool that actually creates belonging.

Belonging is an emotional attachment; it means you matter to the tribe. But we have all been invited to a party out of obligation and knew we weren't really welcome when we got there. A genuine sense of belonging will take much time and effort.

Higher education has been struggling with belonging for some time now and is a great example of the process of an industry working toward antiracism. One example of many is Yale, which is highlighted here not only because of its history but also because of a 2018 incident on campus that goes to the heart of belonging. Yale was founded as an institution for wealthy white Christian men. As time went on, Yale noticed the diversity in society; women and people of color could also learn and pay tuition. The first black student was officially enrolled in the 1850s, but a substantial number of African Americans were not included on campus until 1964.[7]

Yale started including women and people of color slowly (the first woman was enrolled by mistake; she had used her initials and was assumed to be a man). Eventually, Yale successfully got through diversity and inclusion. But the belonging issue was addressed only after an incident in 2018, when police were called on a black female student after she took a nap in her dorm's common room; the complaint to the police had been made by a white student. The black student told the police, who had asked to see her college ID, "I deserve to be here. I pay tuition like everybody else. I'm not going to justify my existence here."[8] That is the voice of someone who does not feel as if she belongs.

Today we speak about equity, which is an important concept because it reflects the ideal of equality as expressed in the 1960s. The problem with equality is that it does not create justice. If we provide equal access to everyone, we ignore the repair needed to actually make people equal. Equity, on the other hand, tries to restore what was lost or never existed and make someone whole—a lofty goal, but not one impossible to achieve. Eyes on are corporate America to lead the way.

Building belonging through equity should be the true intention of an organization's DEI efforts; otherwise, those efforts are unlikely to be successful. Said another way, you can include people of color, but if they don't feel they belong they will not participate fully at work and the benefit of diverse teams will remain elusive. I have heard from countless minority employees who talk about keeping quiet because they don't want to be the one always bringing up race or helping their company be more racially inclusive. So they stay silent, protect their mental state, and try to stay safe in the dominant culture or succumb to cultural hegemony.

How Companies Can Become Antiracist

Equity will increasingly take root as companies, organizations, and institutions become antiracist. While Kendi has many suggestions for how to be an antiracist individual, companies can also proactively become antiracist. Here are a few of his suggested actions that companies can take to shift their culture and see impact, with explanations based on our work with clients.

1. Stop Saying That Your Company Is Not Racist and Admit Racism Exists, and Actively Support Policy to Change That.

When someone says, "I am not a racist," they are letting you know that they don't understand how racism works. The same applies to companies. Companies and organizations hope to dismantle racism, but not being racist is not being American. We can't get away from it. Before the organization's general counsel and HR chief claim that admitting to racism exposes the organization to the risk of lawsuits, reject that CYA notion. Work with legal experts and critical race theorists who can help leaders frame the narrative to take the organization out of the denial of white privilege in a responsible way. Just as with any behavioral change, you first have to admit to having the problem. If your organization has a racial diversity problem, the behavior that needs to be changed is racism.

One company that has started to address its racism is State Street Corporation. Founded in 1792, State Street is a giant in the global financial industry, with $43.7 trillion in assets under management in 2021, making it one of the banks that truly are too big to fail. Because of its size, to say that State Street carries clout among institutional investors, other financial services firms, and the companies in which it invests is putting it mildly. The impact it is making, however, goes well beyond its role as an asset manager and fiduciary. This 232-year-old firm has committed to reviewing and improving its culture to promote greater diversity, equity, and inclusion, both internally at State Street and across the organizations with which it does business. The Lazu Group is honored to support State Street's efforts.

As with so many firms, the wake-up call that something had to change was the George Floyd murder in 2020. But instead of only issuing a statement, State Street's CEO, Ron O'Hanley, made the decision to take tangible and measurable action to further the cause of antiracism. State Street put in place its "10 Actions to Address Racism and Inequality" (discussed in greater detail in chapter 7) to become a more inclusive and diverse organization with the goal of furthering its growth by attracting the best possible talent.

The groundwork had already been put in place with the appointment of Paul Francisco as the firm's first chief diversity officer in 2017. A native of Honduras, Francisco had dreamed of becoming a civil rights lawyer when he was in college, then spent three years in the National Football League before an injury ended his sports career. He joined the corporate world, an experience he has described as a shock when he encountered a sea of mostly white, male faces. Instead of becoming discouraged, Francisco vowed to help change that by working to increase recruitment and retention of diverse talent at companies such as Amica Insurance, Gillette, and Bank of America. He joined State Street in 2011 and, six years later, took charge of a global team driving diversity and inclusion.

In a recent conversation with me, Francisco described taking on the role at State Street: "That was the first time in my career where I saw the power and potential of this work in driving our company forward. Clearly, we still have a lot of work to do, but the fact that I report to my CEO gives me a platform. In this role, I think of myself as a shepherd or steward of this critically important work that is having an impact on 39,000 employees—and an even broader impact outside our organization. It's the first time in my career that I have been truly empowered to do this work."

This is significant and worthy of a callout as a best practice. For diversity work to have the most impact, it cannot be siloed in the Human Resources department. DEI must have a direct connection to the CEO. This makes all the difference in effectiveness, especially when the chief diversity officer is working closely with the heads of departments and divisions. When it is understood that DEI is being undertaken as a business priority at the behest of the CEO, other leaders in the firm have to pay attention. That's when decentralization efforts in DEI work the best (as we explore further in part II). Middle managers understand that DEI is part of the leadership behaviors they are expected to develop and exhibit when managing their teams.

"Before State Street, it was as if I had been puttering along on horseback, riding in the country. Then I joined State Street and, all of a sudden, this Ferrari pulls up and the driver asks, 'You want a ride?'" That was the energy that's put into this position—especially after the Floyd murder—not only for Francisco but for his entire team.

2. Share Your Struggles to Be an Antiracist.
Acting as though you have it all right is a surefire way to get it wrong. You are not going to get it right all the time, and if you try to act as though you do, everyone will know you're lying. While many companies are scared to share their struggles, doing so is actually necessary to see impact from your DEI work. This work requires getting comfortable with becoming uncomfortable, because there is simply no way to engage in this work and not make mistakes. Companies are often wary of being so exposed when they do this work, and individuals may feel that they are all alone, including within their own organizations. But that doesn't mean backing away from the commitment. Undoing the damage from centuries of systemic racism cannot be accomplished in a matter of weeks, months, or even years—particularly if institutional racism is sewn into how a company is set up. It's more than a press release, CEO blog post, or town hall–style meeting about wanting to be part of the solution, or even admitting past mistakes. It's about breaking the norms and challenging the traditions to put an end to systemic racism.

No one should assume that antiracism work is easy or simply requires the flip of a switch in behavior and attitude. It takes courage to stand up against racism in all its forms, including microaggressions, visibly and authentically *within your own organization*. Sharing such struggles is different than admitting liability. The goal is to control the message by getting in front of it. Instead of trying to deal with allegations and lawsuits quietly, companies would do better to mitigate the risk by owning the problem and disclosing actions—before someone else does. Ironically, this level of transparency allows companies to control the narrative, rather than surrender it to other people's disclosure. Center restoration and how the company is changing—that's how organizations can assure diverse communities that the work is actually being done, instead of just checking off boxes.

When I talk to white allies about their lessons learned—such as realizing that they did or said something that was racist—they often describe this as one of the hardest parts of the work. "Shame spiral" is one of the terms that I've heard allies use, in describing the nagging feeling that comes with the fear of being rejected and losing relationships with friends and colleagues of color. What I've found, however, is that when relationships have been established and allyship is viewed as genuine, there is generosity of interpretation in what someone meant to say—and correction is meant to guide, not end further conversations.

My friend Lynne Hoey is chief investment officer of the Kataly Foundation, which supports the economic, political, and cultural power of black and Indigenous communities and all communities of color, and a committed white ally for many years. As she observed in one of our recent conversations: "Shame is not a long-term motivator for continuing this work. . . . It takes owning your story and sharing what you're learning—and that includes how you got here and where you've messed up."

Naming the shame is an important part of the work, as naming it removes some of the sting. As Hoey told me, "Publicly I own my own story—like the times I called one black person by another person's name. I feel the fear but do it anyway. I know there have been times when I put data ahead of the lived experiences of black people. But naming that shame and talking about it helps me."

This is what it takes to value humanity and put compassion and kindness ahead of short-term gains. Instead of leading with an urgent demand for results, companies need to invest the time in truth-telling about past mistakes and the discovery of the cultural values of the communities they belong to. As difficult as this work is, the transformation that follows is profound. Everything else becomes easier and DEI work will be more successful.

Examples of companies going public with their struggles and learning from them are rare, which points to where the real work needs to be done. However, incidents involving the environment and women give us some idea of what it looks like to share struggles and lessons learned. The 2010 BP *Deepwater Horizon* disaster in the Gulf of Mexico has become a textbook case of what *not* to do, including corporate leaders initially downplaying the scope of the catastrophe. More than a decade later the disaster response is being studied by the petroleum industry and policymakers alike to determine what could have been done better, with lessons learned on using science and focusing on containment, which have also helped inform strategy in other urgencies, including COVID-19.[9] In the wake of the #MeToo movement and the revelation of decades of sexual predatory behavior by Hollywood executive Harvey Weinstein, the treatment of women in the workplace finally received the harsh scrutiny this issue deserved. #MeToo gave a voice to many women who felt powerless to fight back and triggered a spate of legislative actions on gender equity in the workplace.[10] #MeToo became a cascading event that not only resulted in the firing of some high-profile men (among them *Today Show* host Matt Lauer)[11] but also middle managers and team leaders, such as at McDonald's restaurants.[12] In companies across the United States, the #MeToo movement required looking at high performers differently, no longer excusing egregious behavior because of high achievement. Today we need the same visibility and accountability in antiracism: owning past and current mistakes, exhibiting vulnerability and visibility on actions being taken, and demonstrating a willingness to take a hard look within at actions and attitudes that need to be exposed and changed.

3. Actively Support Antiracist Policies.
Wringing your hands over racism or shaking your head at the policies passed locally and on the federal level are useless and privileged behaviors. Corporations may like to think that they stay out of politics, but nothing could be further from the truth. Lobbyists show the world just how much power corporations and industries wield. Corporations have long been

active in opposing regulations and social policies they view as costing them money, including gay marriage, equal pay, and a livable minimum wage. If you truly believe in racial justice, then you need to support the policies that promote racial justice.

Seeing conservatives' opposition to critical race theory (CRT) as nothing more than a red herring was something that several companies actually got right.[13] Many corporations publicly opposed the banning of CRT, not only because CRT was not being taught in public schools but also because CRT is important in helping people see they belong by making their history and oppression visible.

The National Basketball Association (NBA) provides an example of a changing industry. What started out as a segregated sport eventually became integrated as NBA leagues opened their doors to black players, who came to dominate the sport as it evolved into a multi-billion-dollar industry. While desegregating the league took several years, within two generations the league had reached the point (in 2022) that 50 percent of its coaches were black. There also were white allies among its coaches.[14]

Golden State Warriors coach Steve Kerr, who led his team to the 2022 NBA championship, is a great example of a leader who speaks out honestly against racism and bigotry. One of the most politically active NBA coaches, Kerr through his behavior has interrupted bigotry. After Floyd's murder, Kerr was very vocal in his support of the Black Lives Matter (BLM) movement and has worked with local organizations, including the Black Organization Project, to convince the Oakland, California, school district to curb police presence on campus. As Kerr told a radio show host, "What I'm learning is you got to listen to the people in the communities that are affected. They're the ones who live the everyday life, they're the ones who know everyone else in the community who understand the problem."[15]

Kerr has been visible, vocal, and consistent in his support for the black community and the BLM movement, and also stands as an example for leaders and organizations everywhere on how to speak out publicly against bigotry. But as with every organization and industry, where there is progress, there is also much more to be done. The NBA, for example, still needs to diversify its ownership. As of this writing, Michael Jordan has been the only black owner of an NBA franchise.

Antiracist policies apply both externally and internally. A case in point is historical sites that have been taking measures to become antiracist and repair the racist false narratives that shaped so much of our learning and acculturation.[16] One of the most visible fights over reparations dragged on for more than two years, fittingly at the birthplace of the U.S. Constitution: the plantation home of James Madison, the fourth American president, known as the father of the Constitution. This story begins in June 2021, when a historic vote by the board of the Montpelier Foundation, which runs Madison's Montpelier plantation historical site, agreed to share governance with the Montpelier Descendants Committee (MDC), which has sought to bring the stories of enslaved people into the mainstream historical narrative. James Albert French, whose ancestors were enslaved at a plantation near Montpelier, chaired the MDC. As he told the *Washington Post,* "No one would have heard of Madison had he not benefited from the 300 people who were enslaved there [at Montpelier]."[17]

The vote by the Montpelier Foundation board to share authority with the MDC was hailed across the United States and internationally as a significant victory, acknowledging the birthright of descendants of enslaved people to help govern a national historical site where their families lived, worked, and died. And then it all fell apart. By early 2022 the Montpelier Foundation had rescinded the vote, which triggered the firing of senior staff who had supported the MDC, including Elizabeth Chew, executive vice president and chief curator of the foundation. Leading the charge against the MDC was Roy Young II, president and CEO of the foundation, and several board members.

According to the *Washington Post,* more than 10,000 people, including donors, signed a petition opposing the board's rescinding of the decision. The National Trust for Historic Preservation, which owns the plantation and leases it to the foundation, warned that breaking the agreement to share governance with the MDC could undermine decades of work. Full-time staff members at Montpelier drafted a resolution for the board, urging support for the original decision to provide at least equal representation for MDC on the board.[18] As a stalemate ensued, a hard-won victory for equity in representation and control of the narrative hung in the balance. With the *Washington Post* following every move as this saga played out, pressure on the foundation board mounted, including loss of funding and other support.

And then things changed again—this time in a positive direction. In May 2022, the Montpelier Foundation board announced that it had voted to accept eleven candidates recommended by the MDC; in addition, Young resigned, and Chew was brought back as interim president and CEO.

The new board was quick to capture the moment by proclaiming Montpelier as the first historical site in the nation to promote equity. But we should never lose sight of how great a battle this was, with broken commitments, intimidation, and a desperate fight to keep white control over a site that once thrived because of the enslavement of black people.

White attempts to own and control cultural heritage happen continuously. Consider the criticism aimed at singer-musician Lizzo after she played President Madison's two-hundred-year-old crystal flute—a gift he received after his second inauguration in 1813. When critics leveled ridiculous complaints that the performance in Washington, D.C., was somehow disrespectful, the Library of Congress highlighted its "routine, necessary practice to loan out historic instruments" and added that Lizzo, like any other artist, had practiced beforehand with the flute and toured the library's collection.[19] It is hard to imagine the critics voicing the same vitriolic comments if a white classical musician had performed with the flute. This was a clear case of cultural racism and bigotry, questioning the ability and integrity of a Grammy Award–winning musician simply because she was a black woman.

4. Speak Out against Bigotry Publicly When You See It.

As discussed earlier in the book, boycotts and consumer activism are shaping corporate behavior and pushing business leaders to speak out against racism and bigotry. Interrupting racism is an essential behavior when becoming an antiracist. Bystander training is an important first step in helping companies get comfortable interrupting racism when they see it. Enabling your culture to be an accomplice in ending racism will make your DEI effective and sustainable.

Speaking out against bigotry, particularly as a privileged white person, is not without cost. Yet to remain silent carries far greater reputational risk. General Mark Milley, the twentieth Chairman of the Joint Chiefs of Staff, faced sharp criticism from Representative Matt Gaetz (R-Fla) about studying CRT in the military. The exchange occurred in 2021 at a House Armed Services Committee hearing to discuss the Defense Department budget for 2022.

"I've read Mao Zedong. I've read Karl Marx. I've read Lenin. That doesn't make me a communist. So what is wrong with understanding—having some situational understanding about the country for which we are here to defend?" Milley said, responding to Gaetz. He added: "And I personally find it offensive that we are accusing the United States military, our general officers, our commissioned, noncommissioned officers of being, quote, 'woke' or something else, because we're studying some theories that are out there."[20] By exercising situational awareness, Milley modeled how to call out bigotry and speak truth to power. If a general, one of the most institutionalized positions of power, finds it important to be honest about race, so can other leaders.

Corporations and other organizations would be wise to pay attention to the discussion around exposing racism and biases, admitting past wrongs, and seeking to make reparations. When a diverse community is welcomed into the discussion, that sense of belonging can lead to healing and a way forward for the future.

From Racist, Not Racist, to Antiracist

Being "not racist" is not enough in the twenty-first century. It means you are still complicit in the institutional, structural, and implicit biases that exist everywhere. Moreover, when you are a leader, this attitude prevents your organization from becoming an antiracist company. Taking the next step to antiracism means admitting your cultural dedication to keeping white people comfortable.

Antiracism is not some esoteric rhetoric; it's the new standard of how companies need to respond to race and racism. It goes beyond putting HR in charge of some initiative to avoid lawsuits. Rather, it means actively and publicly working to dismantle racism in your culture and society. Much more is expected of corporate America today. Doing anything less than the hard work of antiracism will be judged as unacceptable. To have an impact, business needs to engage because antiracism is making the new normal.

II   A Blueprint for Sustainable Change

Organizations today are being called on to actively fight racism. Effecting change takes a blueprint, starting with the understanding that a strong DEI culture enhances profitability and how to think about and set goals. From there, the process unfolds: uncovering cultural barriers, developing strategies to overcome those barriers, decentralizing DEI work, using an authentic voice when expressing DEI work, building connections, partnering with women- and minority-owned business enterprises, and more. It takes a pragmatic approach, with a how-to framework for making meaningful change. But make no mistake: the quest for racial justice, true social inclusion, and equal access to opportunity is highly emotional.

4 From Performative Action to Business Performance

It's not what you don't know that gets you into trouble. It's what you know for sure that just ain't true.

—Mark Twain

The interesting thing about the state of diversity, equity, and inclusion (DEI) in business today is that most people support it, yet progress moves at a glacial pace. This reality seems to blatantly contradict all the pledges, goal setting, hiring of chief diversity officers, and the many other actions that companies have undertaken with much fanfare in the past few years. While corporate performances in the name of DEI may grab a headline, there has been a lack of follow-through, and that has proved detrimental to DEI. With only lip service and no real action, the entrenched opposition remains steeped in white fragility, allowing it to settle in more deeply.

Greg Bensinger, a former member of the *New York Times* editorial board, observed that "we have more work to do," which has become the refrain in one corporate diversity report after another. He added, "If corporate America truly wants to empower the black community and improve diversity, this is the opportunity to make real and lasting commitments to improving hiring practices and the pipeline of talent through corporate initiatives. There are other steps companies should take, including credit guarantees to black-owned businesses to help them secure bank loans."[1] Although Bensinger's observations are spot on, it remains disheartening that, after all the rhetoric and promises about finally addressing racism and bias in the workplace, the *Times* has to publish an editorial to remind corporate America of its own words.

Based on my many years of doing social justice work in communities and in business, I have come to believe that Mark Twain was right. The problem sits in what we believe that just ain't true, as quoted in the epigraph to this chapter. American culture clings fast to the false beliefs that diversity equates to lowering standards, even though it's the opposite. For example, I have never seen a credible (noneugenic) study that showed the benefits of an all-white male executive team. Yet so often in this work, we must constantly articulate the benefits of diverse C-suites. One such proof is McKinsey's aptly named *Diversity Wins* report, which observes that "the business case for gender and ethnic diversity in top teams is stronger than ever," adding that since its first diversity report in 2015, "the likelihood of diverse companies outperforming industry peers on profitability has increased significantly."[2] Tell a business leader that they can significantly increase profits by improving diversity, and it would appear logical that they would jump at a chance to capture that value. Since that's not the case, we can only assume that business leaders either do not believe the stats or they reject the data and are willing to swallow the loss of revenue.

In light of our earlier observations in chapter 2 about reasonable capitalists' desire to make more money, we have to ask ourselves why they are passing up this opportunity to improve their bottom line. The reason, I believe, is that the seemingly good intentions to build diverse teams get lost in years of make-believe around the perils of diversity, resulting in diluted messaging and worrying about legal cases of "reverse racism" against "excluded" white people. Corporations don't have to believe something for it to be true, but if they do not believe in it, their DEI work will remain only performative and superficial, and thus unable to have a positive impact on corporate bottom lines.

For corporate America to achieve a measurable impact with DEI and social justice in proportion to its overarching influence, more must be done, which takes us into the seven stages from intention to impact, as outlined earlier. Since George Floyd's murder, more and more companies have stated their intentions to do something, with a who's who of CEOs denouncing racism and pledging change. This is stage 1 thinking, replete with pledges, committees, and CEO actions of support. But too many companies stop here with this performative action.

It's time to go to the next level, beyond statements of being "dedicated to DEI" and instead actively incorporating antiracism awareness and practices. Stage 2, learning about "the problem," is where most companies move next, and in stage 3 they take obvious actions, such as asking about diversity and inclusion on employee surveys. But the real learning—how to move your company from performative action to business performance and impact—is the goal of this chapter, with more practical advice on implementation throughout part II of this book.

What Performative Action Looks Like

Performative DEI is what makes the headlines, both positive and negative. *Performative* refers to the commitment being a performance—an action or communication that is delivered with a specific audience in mind and meant to spark a particular response. In plain language, it's largely for show. If you are performing or playacting around DEI, you are staying in the first three of the seven stages. You are excited to know the problem can be solved and you are willing to learn and maybe even set some goals to capture low-hanging fruit, but you won't be able to move past the concern and pushback in your company to get to stage 7. This reticence in moving beyond the performative and into performance shows up in the form of leaders pushing back against third-party DEI audits, as happened at JPMorgan Chase. A 2021 shareholder proposal asking the company to conduct a racial equity audit attracted support from nearly 40 percent of shareholders, although the measure was ultimately rejected. The bank's board of directors had recommended rejection of the proposal on the grounds that such an audit would be unnecessary; it already had a "formal accountability" process in place.[3] But 40 percent support from shareholders is hard to ignore. After another shareholder proposal in 2022 called for a third-party audit of its $30 billion, five-year "racial equity commitment," JPMorgan announced it had agreed to retain a third party to perform the audit. While JPMorgan did its share of chest-thumping about embracing equity and inclusion, the real victory seems to rest with the shareholders that pushed for this effort, including the SOC Investment Group. In a statement, SOC's then executive director, Dieter Waizenegger, said, "As support for civil rights and racial equity audits swells across the business world, shareowners expect the nation's most powerful corporations and financial institutions to engage in open and honest assessments of how racism impacts their product and services, not only to protect their long-term interests but to identify new growth areas. We look forward to continuing this dialogue with J.P. Morgan."[4] The bank announced in November 2022 that PricewaterhouseCoopers (PwC) had been retained for the audit, and the DEI community will be watching how far the findings of the audit push one of the largest banks in the world toward greater transparency and progress on racial equity.

Performative action is about window dressing and will not lead to the benefits of outperformance among diverse teams. Without real goals, metrics, and accountability, companies are only playing at DEI. That's what happens when leaders sign pledges but don't commit the budget or the time to implementing those promises. Another common problem is having DEI work sit in the corporate foundation or being viewed only as a cost center and not integral to building the business through improved recruitment and retention of talent and increased revenues and profits. In other words, DEI will remain performative until companies are able to understand its value and properly center DEI as a key strategy to better business performance.

Concerns about the changes necessary to implement DEI start surfacing, and pushback begins to rear its head in stage 4. For example, someone questions messaging or hiring standards, and DEI messages immediately slow down, become diluted. What is happening here is the first encounter with pushback, and you are uncomfortable admitting that your company is racist.

Think back to John Lewis leading civil rights marchers across the Edmund Pettus Bridge in Selma only to encounter a phalanx of white Alabama state police, ready to enforce Governor Wallace's intention of declaring the march illegal.[5] What if Lewis had turned back and said, "Hey guys, they are saying we can't do this. Oh, well, we tried. Let's go home"? Impossible to imagine.

Companies can't afford to let themselves be held back in the early stages. They need to move beyond, although stage 5 ushers in the reality that the pushback is real, while stage 6 admits the pushback is bias. This admission comes with realizations, such as asking the question: Are we slowing down because our managers are centering whiteness? In this moment, at last, you can admit that racism is the most likely answer to what ails your DEI effort. This is where you start to get real about the problem, which will encourage BIPOC employees to feel safe and bring their whole selves to work.

In stage 7, you reach the decision to move around and through the bias. You stop performing DEI and start *being* DEI—diverse, equitable, and inclusive. It is in becoming DEI that you will start to realize the financial benefits.

DEI must evolve by leveraging the knowledge of how equitable processes work and providing clarity on how to replicate those processes throughout an organization. At the same time, organizations must shift their cultures and create systems that can respond to a twenty-first-century context—one of generational realignment and the acknowledgment of systemic failures, from inequities in the criminal justice system to the wealth gap.

By committing to doing more, organizations can take the next step toward making a measurable impact. Stated another way, it's *yes, and* . . .—our shorthand for continuous open dialogue and active listening, while adding the hard work of implementing DEI practices that truly make a difference. The goal is to both change systems and catalyze systemic change.

Think about your culture and your team. Do you have problem raisers or problem solvers when it comes to DEI? Do they come to you with concerns about why it's impossible to center DEI work or are they telling you how the company *can* center DEI work? Honest answers to those questions will show how close an organization is to truly embracing *yes, and* . . . in its approach to taking the first of many steps toward revamping the culture to become more inclusive and equitable.

ESG . . . Connecting Intention to Impact?

Environmental, social, and governance (ESG) initiatives have become the new way for companies to commit to and quantify their good deeds. To attract ESG-minded investors and create a narrative attracting customers and employees, companies are showcasing all the things they are supposedly doing to help the planet and society. All too often, however, a stated ESG focus becomes little more than another check-the-box exercise around waste reduction, improved risk management, and better compliance—all good, but not exactly revolutionary with respect to making substantial improvements. As Harvard Business School professor George Serafeim has observed, "Companies must move beyond box checking and window dressing. In a world that increasingly judges them on their ESG performance, they must look to more fundamental drivers—particularly strategy—to achieve real results and be rewarded for them."[6]

As I observed in the introduction, the real problem, from a DEI perspective, is that the E in ESG receives the overwhelming amount of attention. It's saving the planet by cutting greenhouse gas emissions, reducing energy and water usage, planting trees, and all the rest. While that's laudable—we do need to protect our planet—the E does not stand for "everything," especially at the expense of S. While investment managers focus on E (as in combating climate change) when picking companies to invest in, they should not overlook the social initiatives. But the fact is, environmental improvements are easier to measure—think carbon credits and parts per billion in emissions—than social activism. As Jason Saul, executive director of the Center for Impact Sciences at the University of Chicago and founder and CEO of the Impact Genome Project, has written, "It's time we raise the bar on social impact measurement, create better S data and give the market something to price into their models. It's time to go from net zero to net impact."[7]

The S in ESG may be the hardest, but it's also a blue ocean strategy whereby first-mover companies can set the standard. For many, social activism means supporting philanthropic activities. While it would be great to see more companies standing up for social justice in their actions, speaking out about injustice and inequity, and actively partnering with underserved communities to create more opportunity, they do have to start somewhere. If social change begins with making donations, then at least that is a start. By embracing DEI work to create greater diversity and inclusion within their ranks, more companies may indeed get to the place where they embrace the S as much as the E.

Progressing through the Seven Stages

The journey from intention to impact is not linear. Rather, it progresses incrementally and at different paces at different times. Initiatives can get a jumpstart with momentum generated by commitment at the top, only to become bogged down as implementation proves more challenging, especially at the middle manager level. When the going gets tough, companies face the choice of letting things stall or pushing through. This is the essence of what happens as companies progress through the seven stages from intention to impact.

While no one, in my opinion, has traversed the entire seven stages to declare victory over bias, there are some that are the standard bearers within the corporate world. These are the companies that are moving into the later stages of creating impact around DEI. Here are a few examples:

Johnson & Johnson: Putting Mission into Action

"Our mission is to make diversity, equity & inclusion our way of doing business. We will advance our culture of belonging where open hearts and minds combine to unleash the potential of the brilliant mix of people, in every corner of Johnson & Johnson."[8] Such words alone would have anchored this pharmaceutical giant firmly in the first three stages of making statements and putting an initial spotlight on DEI. J&J, however, has set tangible goals, inside and outside the company:[9]

- By 2025, to have 50 percent of global management positions held by women and 35 percent ethnic and racial diversity in U.S. management positions.

- Also by 2025, to capture 50 percent growth in the number of black and African American employees in U.S. management positions.

- To improve health equity with treatments for HIV and tuberculosis for underserved patient communities.

- J&J also launched its Health Equity Innovation Challenge in Chicago, Detroit, Los Angeles, New Orleans, New York City, and Philadelphia—six cities in which pronounced health inequalities are experienced within black and Hispanic communities. The goal is to listen for ideas from within these communities to improve access to quality care and establish more trust in community-based health care. This initiative is part of its $100 million pledge for communities of color over five years.[10]

For its efforts, J&J has received accolades, including being named one of the "Best-of-the-Best Corporations for Inclusion" by the National LGBT Chamber of Commerce and National Business Inclusion Consortium.[11] By making its goal public, J&J is not just garnering good press, it is also holding itself accountable for hitting those marks. What remains to be seen is how and where it will keep pushing for greater inclusion.

Ralph Lauren Takes on DEI

In the fashion industry, Ralph Lauren is one of the most prominent names, both the designer and the global brand. It is more than label, it is a lifestyle that spans apparel, footwear and accessories, home, fragrance, and hospitality. Years ago, its Polo Ralph Lauren branding had become synonymous with Ivy League prep looks and country club sophistication. Therefore it might be the last company expected to take on DEI in a meaningful way. But that is exactly what Ralph Lauren has done. It is taking a stand as a leader within an industry that, according to the Black in Fashion Council Human Rights Campaign, "is still a far cry from where it needs to be when it comes to diversity and inclusion."[12]

As with many companies, the flashpoint for change at Ralph Lauren was the murder of George Floyd. Three days later, company executives decided they needed to address the pain felt by its 24,000 employees, especially black and African American colleagues. Remote roundtables were convened among employees in sixty-four countries, including those who had been furloughed during the pandemic. Managers were given training sessions ahead of time to support them in listening, rather than jumping in to speak, and to respond with empathy.

Had Ralph Lauren stopped there, it would have been among the many corporations that are satisfied with only the initial phases of DEI work—stages 1, 2, and 3. But Ralph Lauren did more, pushing into the depths of its business and its industry and exposing the very real ways that fashion perpetuates exclusion and bias. This puts Ralph Lauren squarely in stages 4, 5, and 6. As *Vogue Business* observed, "This internal corporate response stands out in an industry that has been slow to address racism, sexism, ageism, ableism and other 'isms.' . . . Weeding out noxious stereotypes, biases and the workplace microaggressions that marginalise employees and customers is profitable according to many analyses, which suggest that diversity in advertising makes it more effective."[13]

Internally, the Ralph Lauren Corporation has doubled down on its DEI efforts by facilitating more dialogue around exposing racism and bias and increasing inclusion, creating safe spaces, and sponsoring DEI councils and teams. Ralph Lauren also has goals to ensure that underrepresented racial and ethnic groups compose at least 20 percent of its global leadership team and to maintain gender parity in leadership at the VP level and above.[14] For the latter goal, the company was the only fashion enterprise on Parity.org's 2022 list of "Best Companies for Women to Advance."[15]

Ralph Lauren's championing of DEI is not only moving the needle within the company, it is also helping to push the fashion industry into difficult conversations about what it means to be inclusive.

Ben & Jerry's Tells It Like It Is

Stages 6 and 7 of the journey from intention to impact are all about pushing in, through, and around obstacles and roadblocks. This is uncomfortable, hard work with truth-telling about a company's goals and aspirations and how and where it falls short. At this level of DEI commitment, Ben & Jerry's stands out among all others. Ben & Jerry's is known for its long-standing commitment to diversity and inclusion; indeed, that has been a guiding principle since the company's founding. This provides the company with an "authentic voice" (as will be discussed in chapter 5) in DEI discussions.

Rather than rest on those laurels, however, Ben & Jerry's takes the higher and more difficult road to continue to explore and expose where it can make improvement. Consider this bold statement:

> Despite the fact that we have long championed racial equity through our activism, Ben & Jerry's remains an overwhelmingly white company. For too long, the linked prosperity we have aspired to create as a business for our workforce and value chain partners has largely left out Black and Brown people. Ben & Jerry's is committed to becoming a truly antiracist company by eliminating racial disparities within the company and to disproportionately creating Black wealth through our business relationships.[16]

As contrary as it might sound, by exposing its shortcomings compared with its long-standing DEI aspirations, Ben & Jerry's has not tarnished its reputation. Rather, it is a refreshing example of a company that sees where the obstacles remain and where it needs to dig in more deeply to change how it does business. If other companies want an example of DEI tenacity—setbacks and flaws and all—Ben & Jerry's is the one to watch.

More Than Just Social

If companies truly embrace the truth that DEI strategies lead to greater creativity, innovation, and opportunity, then these efforts will become sustainable for more than social reasons. Economics are directly linked to DEI. We recall the Citigroup study that found four key racial gaps affecting the black community—in wages, education, housing, and investment—lost the U.S. economy $16 trillion over the past two decades. If those gaps were closed today, $5 trillion would be added to U.S. GDP over the next five years. As the study stated:

> The economic case for closing racial gaps is equally compelling. Present racial gaps in income, housing, education, business ownership and financing, and wealth are derived from centuries of bias and institutionalized segregation, producing not only societal, but also real economic losses. However, future gains from eliminating these gaps are enormous: benefiting not only individuals, but also the broader U.S. economy with positive spillover effects into the global economy.[17]

Impact happens at all levels—from the global to the local, and even the individual. More than ever, consumers are voting with their dollars. They are supporting brands that are aligned with a larger sense of purpose and vision, from ESG goals to greater commitment to DEI and social justice. There is also tremendous potential to be tapped by companies that know how to extend their reach and open new markets by becoming more familiar with and responsive to the needs of diverse consumers. Companies are literally leaving money on the table because they are unaware of the tastes, preferences, and demands of these consumers. Such efforts must extend beyond merely reaching diverse audiences with targeted messaging, such as Spanish-language advertisements to reach Latinx consumers. What is required is more fundamental and ultimately more meaningful: committing the time and effort to understand, engage, and connect with consumers across demographics and markets.

When companies want to hear from employees, a common reaction is to conduct a survey—and it's straight out of the stage 1 playbook of wanting to do something, anything, to show the company's response. It's not uncommon for a company to get high marks initially for "this is a great place to work" or "everyone has a chance to grow here." Such responses, however, more often than not reflect employees' distrust of corporate attempts at feedback gathering, including a disbelief that such surveys really are anonymous. It's safer to tell the company what it wants to hear; after all, what's likely to change, anyway?

This is where discovery groups come in. Using an appreciative inquiry process, tapping into strengths to empower people to contribute to positive change, my firm has been conducting discovery groups for companies and organizations. Most recently, we've been collaborating with organizations to establish a baseline of feedback and commentary from black employees and other colleagues of color, as well as stakeholders, who often feel that their voices are not sufficiently heard or valued. After trust has been established—with assurances that responses are anonymized and not even attendance at the sessions will be disclosed—the barriers start coming down. One person after another will open up, sharing personal experiences about what it's like to work at a particular company, within a specific division, and sometimes for an individual manager. Or, in a different context, people may describe the experience of being a customer, vendor, or other stakeholder. Often, what we hear is that fact finding and other engagement has felt like a check-the-box exercise rather than a sincere effort to listen.

Discovery groups seek to change that impression by facilitating dialogue and sharing among those gathered together. As one person tells their story, someone else is empowered to do the same. People finally feel it is safe to discuss and disclose how invisible and exhausted they feel, how hopeless it is to try to get ahead when promotions continually support the status quo. They speak deep, long-held truths.

Discovery groups should not be mistaken for gripe sessions. Rather, they acknowledge that the people closest to the problems are also closest to the solutions. Their storytelling becomes qualitative data that add depth and nuance to the quantitative data that can be gleaned from employee surveys and workforce statistics. As people drop their armor and become more vulnerable and transparent around their experiences, the company's culture comes into view. Suddenly it's not what the company *says* it is; rather, it's what people feel in their day-to-day interactions with managers, colleagues, and customers. By listening, company leaders can acquire the input they need to pursue desired outcomes, including policy changes, retention programs, and product creation.

One set of discovery groups we conducted was designed to hear from stakeholders how they felt about their city and its responsiveness to planning. One of the concepts we wanted to hear about was resiliency. It was going to be a core response for a twenty-first-century city. When we started to talk about resiliency, we heard from several marginalized communities that the concept of resiliency for them was triggering because it made them recall the constant need for their own social resiliency or the need to be strong. As one person said, "I want my city to help me not have to be resilient." The comment helped us fully understand how using a word we saw as common nomenclature would not have been as well received as the idea of environmental justice.

The best way to ensure DEI actions are not performative is to undertake actions based on what the excluded groups are asking for, not on what you think they need. Finding ways to do that for both employees and customers will move you closer to impactful DEI work. We see that DEI cannot be performative action alone; rather, it can and should be linked directly to accelerating business performance. This requires a willingness to:

- Reexamine talent recruitment and retention. Without diverse talent, companies will find it difficult, if not impossible, to understand and reach diverse consumers.
- Commit to lasting cultural change that will yield successful engagement with new and existing consumer groups.
- Design, develop, test, and deploy new strategies for product development, marketing, and communication.

Such actions need support from the top in order to gain attention and traction. This will only happen with an engaged CEO who recognizes that racism is pervasive and there are biases everywhere. Acknowledging their privilege is often a stumbling block for many executives, particularly CEOs. Most focus on the hard work they have put in and the sacrifices they have made on their journey to the C-suite. Therefore, they find it difficult to identify any advantages they've had or to see themselves as the beneficiaries of any sort of privilege. Yet only by acknowledging how the system has worked in their favor can these leaders identify the impediments to transforming their corporate cultures and doing something about it.

Some effective ways to take action include:

- Coaching, starting at the top, to uncover unconscious biases.
- Identifying systemic problems in hiring, development, and promotion practices.
- Implementing a model of change that is championed at the top and becomes decentralized as it moves throughout business lines, divisions, units, and levels of the organization.

"Unity from Variety"

In 1918, Mary Parker Follett, a management consultant known as the mother of modern management, stated: "Unity, not uniformity, must be our aim. We attain unity from variety. Differences must be integrated, not absorbed, not annihilated."[18] One of the first women to be invited to attend the London School of Economics, Follett brought her ideas about the value of diversity to institutions of economics and democracy. Famed business consultant Peter Drucker once regarded her as his guru, "the brightest star in the management firmament."[19] Yet since then, she has faded into near obscurity, a forgotten business thought leader.

A century ago, Follett was preaching the gospel of empowering others. Inspiring, yes, but also demoralizing when one realizes that we have not made much progress since Follett's days. The persistent challenge has been and remains institutionalized corporate cultures in which values may seem fair but nonetheless perpetuate a white male power structure, such as through prioritizing seniority, requiring certain experience, and engaging in nepotism, all of which make it hard for people from diverse backgrounds to find avenues into a company, let alone follow the pathway to management. In their search for the ideal data set, training programs, or hiring initiatives to end biases, companies are ignoring the fact that most people are still committed emotionally to perpetuating the story of meritocracy, hard work, and a level playing field. It should come as no surprise, then, that equity work has failed because it continues to define a problem rather than solve it.

As a recent *Harvard Business Review* article found, DEI efforts are often shallow, seeking to solve a problem by addressing symptoms—for example, only changing recruitment or making promotions to improve employee demographics, but never tackling the systemic and cultural causes that deeply root racism in corporate culture.[20] Too often, corporate America has no idea how to respond in a way that is authentic and sustainable. What businesses fail to fully grasp is that maintaining the status quo is untenable not only morally and socially but also financially.

If You're Going to Do It, Do It Right

Many companies today are looking for actions they can take to become more inclusive and equitable. But action does not ensure change. In fact, as we've seen, uninformed action can be unproductive and even harmful because it provides a false sense of security that only perpetuates a façade of working toward a solution. The time has come for companies to dig deeper to uncover, understand, and embrace real and sustainable change.

Until we honestly admit that diversity is better for business than the status quo, it will remain elusive. Follett didn't have McKinsey dropping the report, but we do. No business leader consciously makes decisions from a place of denial, but maybe that's why there are so many failed DEI efforts.

As nice as it is to do this work because it is the right thing to do, that's actually disingenuous. Just as people go to work to earn money, businesses are expected to grow and be profitable. To avoid the reputational harm of performative DEI action, companies need to embrace it because this really is a smart business move.

5   Finding Your Company's Authentic Voice

No legacy is so rich as honesty.
—William Shakespeare

Pepsi decided to market to the Black Lives Matter (BLM) movement in 2017 by producing a commercial that depicted celebrity model Kendall Jenner leaving an acting trailer and walking into a BLM protest, where she gave a Pepsi to a cop. Over the years, this commercial has become a classic example of missing the mark. The ad was immediately panned, called everything from blasphemy to an example of what happens when black people are not involved in the decision-making process. Bernice King, daughter of Rev. Dr. Martin Luther King Jr., tweeted, "If only Daddy would have known about the power of #Pepsi," with a black-and-white photo of her father in a protest line while a white police officer bars his way.[1] Pepsi had committed a cardinal sin: the company had entered a conversation it had no place being in.

As the *Washington Post* observed at the time, "It's unclear what message Pepsi's ad was trying to convey. If it was solidarity, critics say it backfired. They say there are ways to embrace diversity in commercials and convey progressive messages without offending the very people companies are trying to attract."[2] For whatever reason, Pepsi apparently thought the commercial would build bridges. However, Pepsi had no legitimacy in building bridges between the BLM movement and cops. The commercial was inauthentic, and Pepsi got pilloried for it.

In *Louder Than Words: Harness the Power of Your Authentic Voice*, author Todd Henry describes an authentic voice as being "sourced in the interplay of your unique passion, skills and experience. . . . Your authentic voice is the expression of your compelling 'why.'"[3] He suggests that, for an individual, an authentic voice is "the expression of identity guided by vision and achieved through mastery."[4] The same applies to organizations. If Pepsi had been authentic in its support for BLM, it would never have made that commercial. Instead, it would have taken the time to learn what allies could do to support the BLM movement, and then translated that into a narrative. Guided by its "why," Pepsi would not have included cops or Kendall Jenner in its ad because it would have been motivated by more than just selling. With an authentic voice, the company would have prioritized respect for the terror in black communities when cops kill black individuals.

For any company to engage in DEI, it must find its authentic voice. That does not happen merely by inserting itself into the conversation, as Pepsi tried to do. Rather, discovering that authenticity starts by looking within, particularly by surveying employee resource groups (ERGs) to identify genuine ways to think about DEI within the company. The company must also invest the time to learn about historical industry bias; otherwise, its message can inadvertently come across as insincere given the industry's track record. In addition, outreach to diverse networks in and around the company's ecosystems will help discover and explore their points of view on diversity.

When a company speaks with its authentic voice, people will be more likely to believe what's being said if that voice ties current values to those held in the past. Consistency matters. When looking at how to integrate different communities, it's best to start with where these communities may feel most welcome. For example, Bank of America sets out a vision that is welcoming to all by posting on its website, "We make financial lives better for our clients and our communities through the power of every connection." This mission speaks to valuing equity ("the power of every connection") while defining *how* that can happen—through improving financial well-being. This speaks to the opportunity of community underwriting and providing banking for the underbanked. If Bank of America wants to speak with a new voice about intentions that become impact, it can find those actions articulated in its vision statement.

Any company seeking to find its authentic voice should create a compensated working group to figure it out. This working group should combine marketing, human resources, ERGs, corporate social responsibility teams, operations, sales, and its foundation. It should be one of the most diverse working groups in the company and ideally should be facilitated by an outside group that is not dependent on the company's hierarchy for success.

To explore more of how that's done, here are three steps to guide companies on finding their authentic voice:

1. Find the DEI Connection to Your Values, and Start There.

Very few companies have exclusionary mission or values statements. Rather, most companies have spent thousands to hundreds of thousands of dollars to develop mission statements that are broad and inspiring. For example, Nike's mission statement is "To bring inspiration and innovation to every athlete* in the world. *If you have a body, you are an athlete."[5] Nike could not be more inclusive than addressing anyone with a body. This gives the company an authentic way to talk to people about athletic gear. But how the company lives this mission is even more critical to seeing whether it's authentic. For Nike there have been some notable wins and losses in this department as it has struggled—but is slowly succeeding—in finding its authentic voice.

Its partnership with National Football League (NFL) quarterback Colin Kaepernick, who led the "take the knee" protest of police brutality during the 2016 football season, is just one example of how the company responded genuinely to a social issue and won.[6] Nike's partnership with Kaepernick helped the company continue to attract black and young consumers. It also speaks powerfully as an example of what companies must do if they want to move from intention to impact.

On the positive side, Nike's brand has successfully attracted diverse audiences. We see it in the company's marketing, such as signing groundbreaking deals, including with National Basketball Association (NBA) superstar Michael Jordan, and keeping Kaepernick after the NFL dropped him and even making him the face of the "Just Do It" campaign for 2018. Nike's sales went up 31 percent in the wake of the Kaepernick ad.[7] While Nike has a long way to go to be equitable, the company starts from a strong place with relationships built within urban communities.

While black people are the backbone of Nike's business model, in the wake of social protests following George Floyd's murder, they called the company out on its hypocrisy for lacking internal diversity. The problem is that Nike's brand was not reflected internally. Like most large international companies, Nike has not moved the needle on racial diversity in its workplace, while its culture has also been questioned.

In 2020, CEO John Donahoe issued a statement to employees: "Our most important priority is to get our own house in order. Simply put, we must continue to foster and grow a culture where diversity, inclusion and belonging is valued and is real. . . . While we have made some progress over the past couple of years, we have a long way to go. I heard this from many of you during my listening and learning tour, and we have heard this loud and clear from you over the past two weeks."[8] As part of Nike's internal reckoning, it began to include DEI work throughout the company, including the appointment of Sam Jarvis as vice president of global diversity and inclusion in 2021. However, after six months in that role, Jarvis left Nike, becoming the third chief diversity officer lost by the company in two years.

Separately, Nike is also exploring accessibility with its FlyEase clothing line with accessible features. Unfortunately, while it says the line was inspired by insights from the disability community, one insight that the company clearly didn't include in the shoe design is that people with disabilities are some of the poorest in America, with 26 percent of the community living in poverty compared to 12 percent of people without disabilities.[9] So when Nike launched the sneaker as a limited edition, it did not think about equity other than in the context of the shoe design. As shoe collectors bought the sneaker, the secondary market of independent sellers made the FlyEase inaccessible to people with disabilities, creating headlines.[10] Imagine if Nike had not made FlyEase a limited edition and instead worked with its foundation to make the shoe equitably accessible. As the FlyEase example shows, while your values are a great place to find your authentic voice, that does not guarantee that you understand what your voice is saying. The hypocrisy inherent in the need for quick wins will come back to haunt you if you don't think things through.

Nike is now taking steps to win both current and future culture wars and make sure its customer base knows. This isn't the first time Nike has moved to change after being continually pressured to be more equitable. One of its first attempts to align its mission and business model was to confront the use of sweatshop labor to build the Nike empire. While it took more than ten years, in 2005 Nike became the first business to publish all its factory contracts.[11]

2. Identify Your Hypocrisy.

You have an authentic voice in your company, and the way to finetune it is to tackle your hypocrisy. In my experience, the financial industry struggles to find its authentic voice. After years of pledges and promises, much remains to be addressed and changed, as "banking while black" incidents continue to occur. In January 2022, Ryan Coogler, who directed the film *Black Panther*, was arrested in a Bank of America branch in Atlanta for trying to withdraw $12,000 from his own account. In an effort to be discreet, Coogler wrote a note on a deposit slip, asking the teller to count the money in another room. Instead, the teller and her manager thought Coogler was trying to rob or scam the bank, and called the police, who handcuffed Coogler until the mistake was realized.

As I wrote in a *Banker & Tradesman* column soon after the incident, there was so much to unpack in this episode. For starters, Coogler is an example of black exceptionalism: a record-breaking, award-winning film director. But what if he had been a no-name black guy who was just trying to be discreet with his money? Would the police have charged him and let the courts work it out? Would he have to prove he wasn't robbing the bank, but only wanted to keep everyone from knowing he was walking out with $12,000?[12]

Consider what happened to Sauntore Thomas, who attempted to deposit the settlement checks he received from a racial discrimination case with a former employer. The assistant manager of a Detroit TCF Bank branch suspected fraud and called the police. Thomas sued the bank for discrimination, received a settlement, and then went on to deposit the checks at a different bank—finally, with no issues.[13] Banking in the black community has been fraught with challenges, and it isn't just a CEO problem. As we'll discuss in chapter 7, it needs to start with better training for the ones who are handing over the money: the tellers, who are usually among the lowest-paid bank employees and yet wield tremendous influence over the customer experience. Without the proper training, tellers can treat certain customers, especially people of color, in a way that makes hypocrisy out of every aspirational marketing and customer service slogan.

The fact is, race in America makes us all hypocrites. This is where the white gaze, or the need to center whiteness and keep white people comfortable, is going to undermine the authenticity of your DEI voice. The reason is the "business side" (e.g., sales) speaks with a language that often still reflects the "old boys' network" and has not yet bought into the business case for greater diversity and inclusion. This will make it doubly hard for companies as they spend time and energy trying to explain away these hypocrisies as being limits of the system. Therefore, deconstructing the hypocrisies will be uncomfortable for some and liberating for others, which is why your voice can't be developed in marketing, alone, and must be driven by DEI true believers.

The rise in labor organizing affords another example of corporate hypocrisy, including Amazon's commercials on how much the company loves its employees. This was an obvious ploy to try to quiet the backlash with employees and their unionizing efforts. But an "Amazon heroes" ad campaign wasn't enough for warehouse employees, who made history in April 2022 on Staten Island, New York, by unionizing after similar efforts in Alabama had failed.[14] (A federal labor judge in January 2023 ruled that Amazon should recognize its first unionized warehouse in the United States.) This started a new groundswell for unionization in other companies as well. Two Starbucks coffee shops in Massachusetts unionized shortly after the Amazon warehouse victory. Hoping to cut off this momentum, in 2022 Starbucks brought back founder Howard Schultz, who traveled the country meeting and talking with employees.[15] Although perceived as an authentic voice for change, Schultz back at the helm is not enough, given his tough, anti-union stance. When asked if he would embrace union representation at Starbucks, Schultz tersely said, "No."[16] But that combative stance is not likely to deter Starbucks workers from continuing to unionize and press for more dignified working conditions and a respectful culture. These efforts continue as of this writing.

Hypocrisy exists. Instead of feeling bad about it, do something about it!

3. Start Quietly until You Find Your Voice—Then Yell!

One of the biggest reputational risks companies face in sharing their DEI voice is not having confidence in it. That's why it's important to start out quietly before yelling from the proverbial rooftops. When you first start to speak out on DEI values, doubts about the sincerity of the commitment may be raised internally and externally; when that happens, it's important that you have a good answer. Take a minute before letting your marketing team run with your new wokeness. Remember that you are not as good at this as you think you are, so don't practice in front of a microphone. Practice with your ERGs, practice with your employees, practice with your investors—then slowly talk to the BIPOC community you are trying to reach.

Once a company finds its authentic voice, it can help connect the dots for stakeholders on why it is taking on a particular issue. A classic example is Ben & Jerry's, which has always been a progressive brand with a long history of taking on social issues. No one was surprised that Ben & Jerry's kept that authentic brand identity even after global conglomerate Unilever bought the ice cream company because customers let Unilever know that Ben & Jerry's authentic voice was a major reason why they bought the ice cream. Activism is a legacy established by the founders, Ben Cohen and Jerry Greenfield, who made social issues part of their vibe, right along with buying milk from local dairy farmers.[17] More than forty years later, Ben & Jerry's then-CEO Matthew McCarthy has described himself as an aspiring activist, under whose leadership the company, even as a Unilever subsidiary, continued to champion progressive causes and values, including LGBTQIA+ rights and racial equality. As McCarthy was quoted as saying in a Columbia Business School profile, "If you know it's the right thing to do, particularly when it comes to nutrition, or health, or safety, you've got to do it. It's my job to make those calls. You have to conspire in organizations. I say that openly, without any sort of hidden agenda. Big organizations have a certain momentum. Some of that momentum is good. Some of that momentum repeats things from the past that are not helpful in moving the organization forward. Sometimes you have to conspire with other like-minded folks in the organization to get stuff done."[18]

While Ben & Jerry's remains the standard bearer of how to use your authentic voice, it's important to remember that Cohen and Greenfield actually believe deeply in this message. The company leadership, past and present, stands ready to take the backlash without getting scared about what it might lose. Your company likely will not start out with this point of view. That's why it's imperative to take it slow, and don't pat yourself on the back for finding your voice; that's not the victory. Rather, the victory is composed of testimonies from authentic community leaders and diverse employees who attest that you do have an authentic voice in DEI.

Once you have that affirming feedback from employees and the BIPOC community, you will know your voice is ringing true. With that solid foundation to stand on, you can get in front of every microphone you can find to evangelize the DEI work and your commitment to it. Even then, some people of color will not trust you, and that's okay. When you're grounded in empathy, you'll remember that their reaction makes perfect sense. Trust takes time, especially after decades—even centuries—of inauthenticity, hypocrisy, and exclusion.

Examples of Sharing Your Voice

While sharing an authentic dedication to DEI may seem hard for companies that center white culture consciously or unconsciously, in companies owned by people of color we often see business models that reflect the desire for equity and justice. There are several examples of this throughout history, from the Southern Tenant Farmers Union, a group of white and black people that first came together in 1934 to protest the treatment of sharecroppers, to the Combahee River Collective, a group of black feminists who have been meeting since 1974 to engage in political work within the group and in cooperation with other progressive groups and movements. As the collective states, "The most general statement of our politics at the present time would be that we are actively committed to struggling against racial, sexual, heterosexual, and class oppression, and see as our particular task the development of integrated analysis and practice based upon the fact that the major systems of oppression are interlocking. The synthesis of these oppressions creates the conditions of our lives. As Black women we see Black feminism as the logical political movement to combat the manifold and simultaneous oppressions that all women of color face."[19]

These examples help shape innovation and progressive agendas among BIPOC businesses. Recently, rappers and entertainers joined the ranks of those investing their money in supporting businesses using similar models and approaches. Among them was the late Nipsey Hussle, who rose to prominence through the West Coast hip-hop scene in the mid-2000s when he released several mixtapes and eventually a Grammy-nominated debut album. Hussle may be better known in his community because of his entrepreneurial efforts, which extend beyond music.

During my time developing economic opportunity, Hussle has been a role model for our work. First, he founded the Marathon clothing line and eventually opened a store, which has been dubbed a "smart store," bridging the gap between fashion and technology through the use of an app. He opened his store in the Hyde Park neighborhood of Los Angeles, which has been described as the center of black commerce in L.A., to provide investment and opportunities in that community. After the success of that store, he went on to purchase the shopping center where the Marathon clothing store is located. As he told *Billboard Magazine* in a 2017 interview, "The concept of the store was something that was a long time coming. Last time I spoke to *Billboard* was for Proud 2 Pay [one of his mixtapes]. I was talking about being a part of the bigger picture of being vertically integrated and be able to deliver products to a retail network that we own and control the experience of, and curate an experience in. So that was the initial seed for the idea."[20]

Hussle also invested in a coworking space and STEM incubator, Vector 90, which was founded by his business partner, David Gross. The vision was for Vector 90 to provide training, professional development, and other tools to help young people of color to launch their own business. In a tribute to the artist and entrepreneur after his death, *NBC News* commented, "Hussle . . . has long had an interest in technology and hoped to bridge the gap between black and brown children in his community and technology entrepreneurs and CEOs in Silicon Valley."[21]

Vector 90 showed us in the inclusive development space that we are on the right track by offering what our community wants and needs to promote greater opportunity. Vector 90 was also a beautiful space and reinforced the need for equity work to be beautiful, dignified, and culturally comfortable. That's why Hussle's death felt like the loss of a trailblazer and inspiration, and we mourned his passing as a loss to all of us.

Another inspiration from the black artist community is Killer Mike, who has a well-known commitment to supporting black-owned businesses. Most recently he bought Greenwood Bank, which he is shifting to a fintech firm with online banking services, catering to the BIPOC community. Killer Mike has attributed his inspiration to conversations with his grandfather, who told him about going to the black dentist, the black doctor, and the black-owned supermarket. For Killer Mike, this idea became a campaign and a three-day social experiment to frequent as many black-owned businesses, some of which had only one to five employees. While on tour, Killer Mike was unable to find a black-owned hotel in Athens, Georgia. Rather than break his commitment, Killer Mike chose to sleep on a park bench.

In my mind, I draw a direct parallel from artists like Nipsey to Harry Belafonte, who decades earlier had done the same thing. I recall a story Belafonte told me about Paul Robeson, famed actor, musician, and activist, who advised him to sing his song, and then tell the people who he was. In Robeson's view during those times, it was not enough to be a successful black. Having crossed over with the following of a white audience, Belafonte's voice had to represent our collective liberation.

It should come as no shock that BIPOC businesses often have more authentic voices on race than white companies. Therefore, it behooves white companies to look to these and other examples to identify and compare the differences in the approach, messaging, and outcomes. White companies should be looking at BIPOC firms for how they engage and create impact as they address their business, their industry, and their community involvement. BIPOC firms show how it is possible to speak with authentic voices holistically, throughout their ecosystems.

Finding your authentic voice in DEI will reduce your reputational risk because you will be speaking your truth, not reinterpreting what you think communities want to hear come from your brand. Authenticity has always been important to building a trusted brand. Being authentic will also allow you to respond more easily to any missteps or missed goals. When people know you are genuinely trying to help, they will give you the generosity of interpretation when you stumble while learning.

6 Goals Alone Do Not Make Change—Uninformed Goals Pose a Reputational Risk

Everyone has a plan until I punch them in the face.
—Mike Tyson

"We will diversify our board." "We are hiring a chief diversity officer to help with talent." "We are opening accounts with black banks." All these statements, reflective of the promises and goals announced by corporate leaders, seemed to have been pulled out of thin air—more reactionary than strategic. Comments such as these could be heard across corporate America in 2020. A *Wall Street Journal* analysis of thirty-five statements and internal memos issued by executives in the week following George Floyd's murder found that most called for unity and condemned racism, although the language used differed.[1]

While public goal setting might appear to be the right thing to do, uninformed action can be dangerous both for communities and for a company's reputation. Goals are intentions; they are public declarations of areas for improvement. DEI goals require systems change to be achieved. Think of it this way: setting a goal is like joining a gym, and if you do not work out regularly you will not see an impact on your bottom or your bottom line. Goals without systems change will not result in impact.

To illustrate, consider the experience of my friend Mike, who a few years ago decided he was going to run the Boston Marathon. It was the year after the terrorist attack at the marathon's finish line, and he wanted to run to show solidarity as well as get healthy. This decision ended up changing Mike's life. As he found, to run 26.2 miles, including the infamous

Heartbreak Hill, Mike had to overhaul his entire routine. He not only started running regularly, he also needed to eat differently and expand his workout to reduce injury and give himself much-needed endurance. He started waking up at 5:00 a.m. for five-mile runs, which changed his morning routine and put much more pressure on his wife to get the kids to school. He changed his eating habits, as well as his kids' diets, which they were not too happy about at first.

Years later, Mike has run five marathons. His daughters join him for his weekend runs, and eating healthily is just what his family does. His intention led to positive change for his whole family. Mike's wife, Sara, sums it up like this: "He was aware and involved in something bigger than himself. He became a better communicator, more present, more patient. He thought he was committing to this one thing, but he was really committing to a lifestyle change."

To reach his goal, Mike had to disrupt a lot of his life and the lives of those he was most accountable to. But the end result is that he is healthier, and so is his family. And as an added bonus, he has raised tens of thousands of dollars for his personal cause, suicide prevention. Mike's story is a smaller, individual story of systems change: in order to reach his desired goal, he had to change his systems and some of the systems of his family.

For organizations, reaching DEI goals will be a similar holistic process. This chapter is about understanding who you actually are so that you can set the most realistic, attainable goals possible. Let's be clear: the goals you set are not as important as what it takes to act on them. Most of the energy is in the preparation to create goals you will hold yourself accountable to, not the actual goals themselves.

Going back to Mike's example, long before he could pursue his goal of running a marathon, he had to commit to preparing his lungs and his joints and to improving his sleeping and eating habits. The bulk of his time and energy had to be committed to a series of holistic goals so that, on the day of the marathon, he could go the distance. In the same way, this chapter is about preparing yourself to set the most honest goals possible. To do so, you will need to accept where you are so that you can chart a course for improvement. Failing to recognize the importance of preparatory goals will be costly. It's like the companies that spend half a year and $500,000 to write one goal, only to discover that it will take six intermediate goals to prepare them to pursue the big goal. If you want to set a goal of hiring 30 percent people of color—then great. But first, start by treating BIPOC colleagues equitably.

This contrasts with using goal setting for a great PR moment, which too often results in these statements being only smoke and mirrors. To paraphrase a Bible quote, "Words without deeds are dead." When creating goals, it is beneficial to identify the systems changes that must be undertaken to reach them, rather than letting your company fumble along without a viable plan. It takes more than trying to adapt old systems with a few new structures.

Setting Goals Starts with Culture

More than 2,200 CEOs and presidents have signed the CEO Action for Diversity and Inclusion pledge to advance diversity and inclusion in the workplace. These organizations embrace a shared belief that DEI is "a societal issue, not a competitive one," requiring "bold action" from the business community and senior leadership to drive change at scale.[2] Spurred by the urgency to respond following Floyd's murder, CEO Action for Diversity and Inclusion is one example of the many ways CEOs have publicly pledged their commitment. Jamie Dimon, CEO of JPMorgan Chase, was quoted as saying Floyd's murder helped him understand that JPMorgan Chase could do more, and the company committed an additional $30 billion over five years to provide what the bank called "economic opportunity to underserved communities," including $8 billion in mortgages for black and Latinx households.[3]

Across the corporate landscape, much has been said about the need to increase DEI, particularly in industries such as technology and financial services that have traditionally been dominated by white males. Both industries have made pledges to improve their diversity scores, with tech being particularly vocal. According to *Fast Company*, a survey of forty-two leading tech companies revealed nearly $4 billion had been committed to DEI.[4] However, a recently published report provided evidence that tech continues to lag its intentions to improve workforce DEI. In a survey of 2,030 workers, 50 percent of respondents said they had left or wanted to leave their job in tech or IT, citing a culture that made them feel unwelcome or uncomfortable. More than half of women, Asian, Black, and Hispanic respondents said they had these experiences.[5] These disappointing results counter the statements made by tech companies that they would both increase diversity within their ranks and also commit to DEI, in the wake of the social protests following the Floyd murder.

In financial services, the story is much the same. Although white women have been making inroads, for people of color there is a noted lack of opportunity and upward mobility. McKinsey observed, "Indeed, our data show that racial and ethnic identity—Asian, Black, Latinx, and white–play a major role in the experience an employee will have, particularly in the financial-services sector. Representation in financial services is especially effective for achieving equity, since the sector has control over capital and assets that yield outsize power and influence over markets, the business landscape, and entrepreneurship." McKinsey went on to give pointed advice to companies: engage in the "significant work left to do" so that people of color will have equal opportunity for success.[6]

Goal setting must be grounded in a supportive culture. (This is so important there is a whole chapter on shifting culture later in the book.) The takeaway here is that for any goal to succeed, culture must shift first. For example, if you value the fact that your board members all have Ivy League backgrounds, you may think that taking someone from another university will dilute your board effectiveness, but I assure you, it won't. Instead, it will guard against group think. Every university has a brand, and if you have a roomful of people who share one background, you'll have more of the same; discussions will constantly devolve into an echo chamber.

Setting Goals for Success

It is not enough for companies to *talk* about it; they need to *be* about it, and that starts with setting goals. To do that, it is critical for any company to have tools in place to position its management and staff for success. It's all about how to move from goal setting (intention) to effort activation (impact). Before you set goals, there is some prework to do. After all, you may not know enough about equity to set goals that make sense or that will lead to impact. Just as you need market research before you set sales goals, you need to understand diversity in context to set DEI goals.

Find the courage to ask yourself: Do you actually believe that diversity is a strong business imperative? And if not, is this opinion coming from your head or your heart? The data are clearly saying DEI is how you should lead your company, so if you do not believe the data, you should probably not be the one leading this work.

As discussed, George Floyd's murder led to a widespread desire among many companies to respond with commitments to greater diversity, equity, and inclusion; however, the realities of succession planning and a company's commitment to seniority may actually make that impossible to achieve in the next twenty-five years. For example, imagine if the year *before* social protests over DEI your company promoted some promising young men to the C-suite. Because of their age, these executives will likely hold those positions for a generation regardless of any subsequent intentions to change things moving forward.

Ask yourself and your team this fundamental question: *Why are we setting DEI goals?* Reactionary goals are hard to keep, which makes a proactive approach all the more important. Take some time to figure out how diversity can authentically help your company. Get narrow and specific around how diversity will help future-proof your company. You should be able to articulate how diversity will give your company a competitive advantage.

For example, PepsiCo seems to be handling entering the Latinx community with more grace than the BLM conversation. PepsiCo has established stand-alone businesses in both food and beverages to address the Hispanic market, with a goal of opening new markets and serving more customers. Recognizing this opportunity, PepsiCo didn't just view the market as a monolith; it knew a monolithic strategy would not work. Instead, the Hispanic market represented many different groups and types of consumers. In an interview with *Beverage Digest*, Esperanza Teasdale, the vice president and general manager of PepsiCo's Hispanic Business Unit for beverages, said, "There are so many ethnicities within the Hispanic consumer base that approaching them as one monolithic group is not ideal. While there are similar values, there are different cultures. There's different food, music, and local traditions that make Hispanics much more unique than just saying 'Let's just communicate in Spanish and we got everybody.' We have multiple cohorts." To succeed in its overarching goal, PepsiCo needed to deconstruct the monolith and identify individual goals to understand and appeal to each targeted customer segment.

Question Norms and Traditions

Why haven't we been able to become diverse naturally? This is a hard question that requires questioning norms and traditions that may be sacrosanct within a company's culture. It may be that a company's definition of meritocracy is fraught with bias and is really more about similarity of experiences rather than accomplishments. "Cultural fit" could be a term used to eliminate qualified talent. Whatever the underlying truths, it is important to understand why your company has not embraced greater diversity.

In *Mediocre: The Dangerous Legacy of White Male America*, author Ijeoma Oluo paints a picture of "white supremacy" that is not limited to "Klan members and Neo-Nazis." She writes, "Blatant racial terrorists—while deadly and horrifying—have never been the primary threat to people of color in America. It's more insidious than that. I am talking about the ways our schoolrooms, politics, popular culture, boardrooms, and more all prioritize the white race over other races. Ours is a society where white culture is normalized and universalized, while cultures of color are demonized, exotified, or erased."[7] When corporate culture mirrors the social norms as a whole, we should not be surprised that companies have a distinct lack of racial and ethnic diversity.

Oluo also traces the history of women exiting the workforce, presenting it as part of her thesis of white mediocrity. As World War II came to a close, many women and their employers did not want women to leave the workforce. However, men were returning from the war, and the government was worried about high unemployment among the white GIs after they came home. The military worked with women's magazines to encourage women to leave the workplace.[8] Such actions go a long way toward explaining why women have not historically been in the upper ranks of companies: the government and corporate America decided to prioritize the employment of white men coming home from war over everyone else. As this example shows, historical bias will always be part of the answer, but so will your culture, industry, and implicit bias.

Confront White Fragility

What do I need to know as a leader to lead responsibly, toward impact? Answering this question starts with being vulnerable and candid with yourself and others about being genuinely committed to making an impact. Ask yourself: Am I comfortable talking about race, and, more important, am I comfortable talking about white privilege? Reaching your employees and customers authentically means you need to show them how you understand their problems, and white privilege is one of the largest.

In her book, *How to Be Less Stupid about Race*, Crystal M. Fleming explains that race is "fundamentally a stupid idea," and America has been doing "philosophical acrobatics to have it make sense within the narrative of democracy, meritocracy," as well as the U.S. economy.[9] The solution, she says, is to "dismantle the system of unearned privilege attached to being socially defined as 'white.'" Fleming exposes white supremacy as a "system of power designed to channel resources to people socially defined as white."[10] Similar to Oluo, Fleming sees white supremacy as "the way our society has come to be structured such that political, economic and other forms of capital are predominantly maintained by elite whites." Fleming calls for a shift of consciousness around whiteness.

There is a far distance between what Oluo, Fleming, and others see as the necessary hard work of reparation in society and business culture and the reality of where corporate America is today. Getting comfortable with diversity work takes experience, and most business leaders have little or no experience in this new world. When they hear the term *equity*, they think about ownership rather than justice. Just as with any other business proposition, it's what you don't know that will kill you. The best advice here is to be proactive, especially when it comes to talking to black and brown business leaders to gain insights into the culture you are inviting into your company. Talk to white allies who can help you understand how to lead successfully on these third rails of America. Organizations such as Showing Up for Racial Justice (SURJ) is a great one to help get you started.

When companies take the time to build relationships with communities (particularly those that are underserved), goals become more realistic and achievable. Most important, the goals will actually be meaningful to the community because they are responsive to the community's needs. For example, I can think of several financial institutions—from credit unions to large, publicly traded banks—that are working toward attracting women- and minority-owned business enterprises (WMBEs). It starts with getting to know the communities in real time. One particular financial institution brought in small businesses to speak directly to credit officers and business bankers to share input about what they need from a banking relationship. Hearing about these needs caused the bank to create specific products and services for their customers.

An example is the Self-Help Credit Union, which operates in California, North Carolina, South Carolina, Florida, and Virginia. It focuses on people of color, women, rural residents, and low-wealth families, seeking to enable and empower them in ownership and economic opportunity. Working with Runway, a community underwriting product, Self-Help Credit Union is investing in community underwriting in a participative model that is close to the community. And seeing results, after two years of providing more than $700,000 in community-underwritten loans, more than 145 jobs have been created in the Bay area. In my view, this is a far superior approach to building banking relationships with WMBEs than is repackaging loans with a lower credit score and calling it WMBE banking.

Let BIPOCS Lead and Support White Ally Work

In order for your goals to be relevant and meaningful, it is important that the people who are closest to the problem be the closest to the goal setting. Therefore, letting BIPOCs lead while white allies provide support is the most effective strategy. Let's be clear here: leading does not mean all face and no responsibility. Leading means having the power to greenlight efforts and hold people accountable. As a woman of color who does honest DEI work with companies, I can see hesitation in clients at times to let me lead with honesty, which gets exacerbated by the business need to continue my contracts with them. It would be so much easier to tell my clients their current efforts are great, rather than tell them the truth—that many efforts are a waste of money and risk losing the contract. However, if they trust me, they will let me guide them on this journey. And their letting me do that leads to meaningful change that can take place on many levels.

A great example of this in action is Congresswoman Ayanna Pressley of Massachusetts, who beat a twenty-plus-year incumbent by reminding her constituents that representation matters. It is great that former congressman Capuano was willing to vote to support people of color, but that is not the same as BIPOC representation. As Pressley says, "The people closest to the pain, should be the closest to the power, driving [and] informing the policymaking."[11]

The fact is, you will get a different perspective and more impact when communities of color lead the work, and that includes the consultants you hire and the employees who are empowered to fully participate in DEI discussions. This will also be the first time most of your white employees and managers have been led by people of color, an important practice for creating a more equitable culture. Now here is where you must get nuanced. Letting the BIPOC community lead does *not* mean dropping the responsibility of DEI on the shoulders of BIPOC employees, who are most likely tired of being the few "others" in a company and may resent the request. Be open for them to decline this task. If they are taking on the responsibility, they should be compensated for it, and they should have BIPOC experts working with them.

At the same time, if you want to achieve DEI goals, white discomfort will need to be addressed. In her book, *White Fragility*, Robin DiAngelo helps the white community identify the vulnerability they feel when dealing with race. White fragility, as she defines it, is the defensiveness and discomfort white people feel when looking at racial injustice.[12] It is why C. J., my Alabama host from chapter 3, wanted to tell me his parents did not own slaves.

Providing a safe and brave space, supported by white allies, will help organizations handle white discomfort internally. White diversity consultants can help hold space for the discomfort white people will naturally feel. And creating a white ally employee resource group (ERG) can help white employees who want to become better allies support one another. However, it is important not to center white discomfort; rather, the objective is to create a space for people to work through it without distracting from the larger work. For example, IBM president Thomas Watson Jr. set a standard for white allyship in the early 1950s as IBM sought to build manufacturing plants in North Carolina and Kentucky. Watson said at the time he wondered how his intention to racially integrate the plants would be viewed by the states. Nevertheless, he wrote in a September 21, 1953, letter, "It is the policy of this organization to hire people who have the personality, talent and background necessary to fill a given job, regardless of race, color or creed."[13]

Watson Jr.'s letter continued to uphold the values of allyship and equity started by his father, Thomas Watson Sr. In 1935, Watson Sr., who was then chairman and CEO of IBM, stated that men and women doing the same kind of work would receive equal pay and treatment, and the same opportunities for advancement. This became a legacy and a standard. In its 2020 diversity report, covering more than ninety countries, IBM reported it was addressing pay gaps based on gender, race, and ethnicity. This is not charity; as IBM chairman and CEO Arvind Krishna said in the report, "Diversity and inclusion are key to our company's success and can help propel innovation and expand access to opportunity."[14]

From this legacy of championing diversity, IBM has become recognized for its DEI efforts, including providing more opportunities for women and people of color and emphasizing supplier diversity—all of which it sees as a business imperative.

Another example can be found at State Street. Lou Maiuri, president and head of investment services, has taken a strong stand on DEI. As he wrote in his blog, "Engaging head-on with DE&I issues helps us better understand and reflect our clients, stakeholders, and the communities in which we operate. Diversity is critical for innovation. It challenges groupthink, and ensures we have perspectives that produce more equitable solutions."[15] However, he also noticed that talent retention among people of color—specifically black employees—was not where he wanted it to be. As business leaders know, the cost of talent turnover can be measured in money, instability, and loss of relationships. Retaining diverse talent is key to businesses remaining highly relevant to their clients.

When it came to improving retention at State Street, the way forward was not clear. So Maiuri started a workstream to gain insights and find some answers. My firm partnered with members of State Street's Black Professional Group and Black Leadership Cohort to take on this business challenge, namely, to discuss issues surrounding recruiting and hiring, professional development, and retention of black talent, particularly at the seniormost levels. As Maiuri wrote: "During our half-day session, the feedback was candid and detailed, humbling and revelatory, raw and poignant. I spent most of the half-day session listening and learning so I could identify opportunities to drive change and deliver meaningful results—to turn our intentions into action."[16] Most important, this wasn't approached as "one and done." The process continues as these groups have been convened again to discuss progress and provide more feedback as we continue forging the way ahead.

There is a significant takeaway here: Once you have grounded yourself in ways your company will need to change in order to achieve DEI objectives, goals need to be set deliberately and with intention. Sit with each one and think about how you would go about implementing these desired behaviors and best practices into your plans and operations. Otherwise your goals will likely not be reached, and you will open yourself up to reputation risk.

Tie DEI Goals to Bonuses

As the adage states, to change something you first have to measure it. But I take it one step further: if you want to guarantee change, you must tie the metrics to bonuses. One of the biggest differences between my time as a social justice activist and my current work in the private sector is money. When working for nonprofits, you are incentivized by the change you are making in the world and the relationships you are building. It is more than money; it is that "bigger than yourself" feeling you get when you know you are doing something for the larger community, such as feeding the hungry or protecting children.

In a corporation, however, the most potent incentive is money. There is no need to pretend otherwise. If you want your talent to reach DEI goals, tie it to people's bonuses and give them all the support they need to reach them. While you may be nervous about tying DEI to bonuses, it's actually much easier if you are not selling DEI as charity but as a business imperative to help the company maintain relevance. IBM is among the companies that holds its executives accountable in this way, including by tying their bonuses and compensation to achieving progress on DEI goals.[17]

Create a Cross-Departmental, Cross-Level Committee on Equity

Many companies have committees dedicated to equity and diversity, but often they are siloed and separate from each other. They sit in HR, which usually has little incentive to work closely with the business side. They sit in marketing, which focuses on product campaigns. They sit in ERGs, which create connections among employees. But these groups do not necessarily talk to each other, nor does their work become symbiotic in the greater service of DEI. When such siloes break down, however, meeting and working on goals and communications together will strengthen the company's culture and encourage all levels of a company to cocreate the way forward.

Some of the best information is sitting in the bottom of your company's pyramid because that's where people of color are. But it is also where different education and experiences sit. To tap those insights, companies can create DEI committees for the board, the company, and ERGs. When these groups meet regularly with each other, an open line of communication is established from the ERGs to the board of directors. The board can get dispatches from the streets, if you will, which could better support strategy integration and evaluate the work.

Prepare and Evolve Middle Management

Middle managers are some of your truest believers. They are people who have dedicated themselves to a company and worked their way up. However, middle managers have succeeded in the current structure, and to them, the changes brought by DEI may feel as though the goal post is moving, especially for their own career advancement. Giving middle managers education and support first will make any effort more effective. If middle managers are excited, they will manage their teams to reach their goals. It's a message I tell my clients repeatedly (and I say throughout this book): middle management will make or break DEI efforts, which is why this work needs to be decentralized.

Though change starts at the top, it is implemented through the middle; therefore, any of your goals will be interpreted by your managers, who may not believe in it as much as you do. A great example of how managers can kill your DEI goals is the Bank of America lawsuit and settlement. In 2011 came the mother lode of fines: Bank of America paid $335 million because of accusations of discrimination against qualified black and Hispanic borrowers. Bank of America's Countrywide Financial subsidiary was accused of unfair lending practices, including allegedly charging higher mortgage fees to black and Hispanic borrowers compared to white counterparts. Though Bank of America paid up, it denied that it had practiced racial discrimination. Then, in 2013, Bank of America paid more than $2 million to settle allegations of discrimination against black job applicants, and in 2019 it paid $4.2 million to settle other discrimination claims. The point is, racism shows up on the front lines, where staff meets with customers. It's the same in bank branches as it is in Starbucks stores.[18] Because the fact is, companies may not discriminate, but managers and their decisions could. And when racism shows up on the front lines, it affects the bottom line.

Open Communications across the Enterprise

Any DEI goals will create some concern for employees; therefore, open communication is critical, not just around the goals themselves but specifically as to how these goals will benefit the company and how management and employees will be supported in reaching these goals. As Deloitte observed, "Leaders owe it to both their organizations and individuals to communicate the importance of DEI early and often. Effective DEI strategic communications help individuals embrace new beliefs and behaviors ultimately supporting a shift in organizational culture that fosters equity and belonging."[19]

If the employees are white, there is a 75 percent chance they do not have friendships with any nonwhite people;[20] therefore, providing them with goals without also providing them with access to new networks and ways to build new relationships is unfair. Unfortunately, it is often the case that employees and managers discuss these changes without enough information to put in place informed strategy.

You have to communicate the value of diversity and reinforce why the business is missing opportunities because of its narrow definitions and situational awareness. Remember, most people do not have experience with diversity; for them, it is a complete unknown. Rather than run from uncomfortable questions from employees such as "Will you hire less-qualified people if they are people of color?," be open to these questions and answer them. Explain that this belief of hiring "less qualified" is due to bias, and people of color are an untapped market, many of whom are sitting in positions for which they are actually overqualified. Introduce them to historically black colleges and universities and college affinity networks so that they can see the pipeline of talent. Remind them that the most educated demographic in America right now is black women. Dedicated educational communications on DEI companywide will help the company understand how to connect leadership to this effort.

As this discussion shows, goal setting is the start. Do not set these goals for public relations purposes; rather, set them because your company is ready to enter and seize its future. As with any other goal, you need the capacity to reach it despite the inevitable barriers that will impede progress. It is also important to understand how priorities will need to shift within the company. While reaching DEI goals represents a tremendous investment of time, energy, and money, not reaching them will be even more costly.

Thinking about Goal Setting Differently

To this point, we have not said much about setting goals; rather, all our efforts have focused on the prework. Admittedly, this flies in the face of the traditional approach to goal setting, which wants to jump in to do something. I hear this all the time from clients: Should goals be realistic or aspirational? Quantitative or qualitative? Should we have a short or a long time frame for implementation? The answer: yes! You're going to need all that and more. But that's not the starting point.

So much of DEI work is subjective because it depends on a number of variables, from how biased an organization really is to how risk averse it is when it comes to change. Leaping into goal setting without looking at that reality will result in a lot of wasted time, effort, and resources, as well as yet another ineffective DEI strategy. It's time to look at goals differently.

First, start by *reworking the existing goals* to be more equitable by viewing them through a DEI lens. Doing this means taking on what has been considered sacrosanct within the company—unwritten rules, how things get done, who has the power. It means looking at policies around hiring and promotion, looking at strategies for relating to diverse customers. (We'll discuss this in greater depth when we take up the workplace culture in chapter 7.)

Second, focus on the goals that affect the bottom line of your business, everything from sales to R&D—not just HR. Doing so links DEI directly to business priorities. Everyone in the organization must understand that pursuing DEI goals will lead to everyone, including white colleagues, making more money. This will help create more buy-in.

Third, think about communication and how the message is delivered and received. For example, when the organization sets a goal of hiring more people of color, do people hear the aforementioned faulty assumption, "We will hire less-qualified people to get diversity"—a view that literally makes an imaginary white person more qualified than an imaginary person of color? DEI is about more; it is about equity, opportunity, and a sense of belonging for everyone. Bringing that message home will require goals that center changes in white attitudes as much as they center diversity. Goals cannot just be quantitative and numeric, counting the number of people of color in the organization and at every rank and level. Goals need to also be qualitative around the experience within an organization, especially centering white allyship.

Start with where you are; there is plenty of work to be done there. Then goals can shift from the realistic to the aspirational on a foundation of incremental progress.

Fighting the Good Fight

This chapter opened with a quotation from Mike Tyson: "Everyone has a plan until I punch them in the face." That might have seemed surprising in a chapter on goal setting. But there is much truth in those few words. Every boxer who has ever faced Tyson has entered the ring with a goal and a plan to beat him—except his punch was devastating.

Racism is the same, a formidable opponent that is entrenched and ingrained throughout organizations, in policies, practices, and protocols. Its strengths undermine the achievement of goals, sometimes making a mockery of them. The key—indeed, the only hope—is in the preparation to take on DEI work: by practicing taking the punches, building strength, and protecting vulnerabilities. This is both the prework and the constant work. And that's how we keep fighting the good fight.

7 Creating a Curious Work Culture

Success comes from curiosity, concentration, perseverance, and self-criticism.
—Albert Einstein

It was 2010, and I had become a burned-out organizer trying to stop the justice system from criminalizing young boys and girls of color. No matter how hard we worked, we couldn't seem to make any progress. Everywhere I turned there were barriers and obstacles; even when invisible, they were insurmountable. And then I came across a quotation from Peter Drucker: "Culture eats strategy for breakfast."

I read and reread those words, and after about the fifth time I started to cry, not just tearing up but snotty, ugly crying. Drucker's five words changed the course of my work forever. As a community organizer working in twenty-six states, I was trying to get America to adopt a strategy that was incompatible with a culture that only knew how to criminalize black boys and girls, a culture that accepted that blacks are 3.23 times more likely than whites to be killed by police.[1] I had spent years thinking the only reason we were not changing that brutal fact was because we didn't have the right strategy, and that once we finally found it, we just needed to ensure we had sufficient time and money to implement the strategy. Drucker's words, however, rang like truth in my heart, helping me realize that the dominant culture in America was swallowing the sound strategies that would decriminalize the system and spitting them back out as diluted, ineffective change. It showed up in blaming voters for not voting rather than acknowledging the understandable distrust of democracy by people who have been excluded by the system, as well as in voter suppression and other efforts (moving polling places, purging voter rolls) meant to disenfranchise people.

From my time as an organizer, I took this sobering realization and Drucker's words and brought them into my work with business organizations. The message I deliver, time and again, is that even the biggest and best strategies for DEI will get eaten up in middle management and lost amid other aspects of work culture. A perfect example is how biased processes get embedded in meritocracy cultures that reward the status quo, without acknowledging how the broader base of highly qualified, diverse talent is overlooked. This is the starting place to set up any DEI effort for success: knowing there are elements in your culture that will stop a DEI strategy from being implemented.

When I deliver that message to clients, I'm often greeted with assurances such as "our culture embraces diversity." But the words in a mission or values statement are not sufficient to excavate and eliminate biases, conscious and unconscious, that have existed within a culture for years—even back to the founding of the company.

There are many definitions of culture. Broadly, culture can be considered a set of shared norms, values, traditions, beliefs, arts, and behaviors across a particular group of people.[2] Communication in all its forms—oral, written, visual, and nonverbal—reflects the cultural fabric and patterns of groups and organizations. Those cultural patterns include how people attach value to objectives, achievements, status, ideas. The more entrenched these signs and symbols are, the more they become part of the norm that is revered to the point of being unquestioned. Their influence cannot be overestimated because they define how people view themselves and their standing within an organization or society.

Business culture is rooted in an organization's history and traditions, including the beliefs and behaviors that guide shared assumptions and norms accepted by the group.[3] The culture of an organization may have taken root decades, even centuries, ago and continued through current management. Examples include health care companies that are rooted in discovery and improving health, or industrial companies that tout a legacy of ingenuity and powering progress. The same applies to startups, which by and large reflect the mission and vision of the founder. Over time, culture becomes institutionalized, with policies, procedures, and systems in place, such as those for hiring, promoting, and compensating people. Values become codified and let people know what matters most, whether that's innovation in a "break things" culture or compliance in a more buttoned-down environment.

Regulations and other external factors also shape a business and its culture. For example, in banking, regulations interject values, such as protecting people from fraud or predatory practices. In utilities or manufacturing, safety and security concerns impose expectations for how operations will run.

Over time, business models are created to serve customers with products and services. Often these become inextricably linked with culture as consumers equate the products they use with the brand, and therefore the company. Apple is a perfect example of this, with its products, name, and logo homogenizing into a single experience.

Similarly, investors and their expectations can shape culture. An example is the current trend in environmental, social, and governance (ESG) investing, which at best encourages genuine strides toward sustainability and at worst is only greenwashing to provide the appearance of it. Not all investor interests align, however, as the culture of private capital investing puts an unblinking focus on generating a return, which is often diametrically opposed to social impact investing that seeks to do good as opposed to only doing well.

To create a culture in which diversity is truly valued, an organization needs to develop a curious culture. People become genuinely more curious to learn about and connect with others instead of just being concerned about losing their power or position within a company. And that's where this discussion begins: defining curiosity in this context and examining why it is important for cultural change.

The Power of Curiosity

When Harry Belafonte was invited to the White House by President John F. Kennedy, he was unsure whether he should go and, if he did, what he should do or say. He sought the counsel of Dr. Martin Luther King Jr., who knew the importance of Belafonte going. King said to him, "Find his moral center and win him to our cause." Belafonte often repeated this story in front of investors and donors to remind them of their moral center. He obviously helped win Kennedy to the cause and did it through being curious about his values. In turn, Kennedy became more curious about black people and their experience in America, including the need for greater inclusion. That's the power of curiosity.

In their 2015 book, *The Power of Curiosity: How to Have Real Conversations That Create Collaboration, Innovation and Understanding*, Kristen Siggins and Kathy Taberner suggest that curiosity is "being inquisitive, seeking to learn and understand," and can "help us successfully navigate our transition from the hierarchical Industrial Age to the more collaborative Information Age."[4] This idea can be extended to the collaborative nature of DEI work and our transition from the racist times of the Industrial Age to the more collaborative times of equity and justice. Curiosity is essential, promoting genuine interest in others and their experiences.

One big distinction Siggins and Taberner draw is between being curious and being nosy. Being nosy is about judging and comparing, with the intent "not to learn but to compare, perhaps wanting to determine who is better or worse."[5] We all probably have that neighbor or older relative who asks us how we're doing but really is just digging for details (and sometimes dirt). For example, after my friend's sister died, community members began inquiring about care for her special needs child, not because of wanting to help but to see if they could fault the arrangements the family was making. This happens in corporations as well as in communities.

In suggesting a new communication paradigm, one that moves from telling and judging to asking and accepting, a company sets a standard that does not seek to blame or exclude other perspectives. Rather, by promoting curiosity, a company can establish a culture anchored in belonging. This allows us to imagine the cohesion and emotional satisfaction that can be generated when white ignorance is undone by curiosity. This calls to mind a recent MIT talk I participated in on the Cherokee Nation's cultural values, which include curiosity grounded in respect. As Wahde Galisgewi, who has developed adult immersion language revitalization programs for the Cherokee Nation, observed, "When a Cherokee is faced with a problem or challenge, the first thing they do is ask questions. They're not pushy or nosy, but they want to know what other people think, so they're curious in a very respectful way."[6] However, white culture, or the idea that whiteness is the "norm," can stymie even the best-intended DEI initiatives because people feel they must censor themselves. It takes dramatic, even drastic, measures to provide safety for underrepresented employees to speak truth to power.

That was essentially what my firm needed to create during a discovery meeting we conducted for several black employees of a company, since the event was also attended by two white executives. As the discussion got underway, the black employees settled into a comfortable banter with each other. Barriers came crashing down as people became more candid about what it feels like to be black in corporate America today. Among peers whose experiences mirrored each other's, there was no need to filter their reactions and comments. People began saying things they could never say in a room that was majority white.

As they listened to their discussion from the back of the room, the two white executives, both of whom consider themselves to be empathetic and aware, were privy to comments they'd never heard before. They understood, probably for the first time, that black employees filter themselves at work every day and feel as though they have to constantly explain themselves to white colleagues who seem to lack the curiosity to translate a different experience into their own understanding. In other words, they live and work in the glare of the white gaze.

Then the conversation became even more real as the black employees engaged with the executives, making honest statements such as: "We know you are trying, but the truth is we want to see black people moving into jobs like yours." It was an eye-opener as these executives acknowledged the impact of having an all-white senior team. It wasn't enough to try to improve diversity and inclusion at the lower and mid-levels of the organization; pathways needed to be established and opened for black talent to have greater opportunity to rise to positions of authority and influence.

After the meeting, one executive, visibly shaken, told me, "They're right; I never realized it before." For the first time, this executive truly felt empathy and a deeper connection with black colleagues than ever before. The executive also took responsibility for perpetuating a white-centered system even though leadership was trying to change it.

When the barriers come down and people get real, cultural shifts can happen. But this requires a level of vulnerability and transparency that many in corporate America will find uncomfortable, even untenable.

As this story about the discovery meeting shows, organizations cannot move from intention to impact without shifting their culture. This is hard work because the culture predates the individuals who are trying to make this change. So many parts of the culture that exclude people will feel like

traditions, philosophy, or norms. As Charles Mills observes, only by identifying and eliminating such structures can we eradicate white racial privilege.[7] One structure I've cited before is seniority, which on the surface often
seems like a rational criterion for promotion. However, it actually slows
down diversity by prioritizing people who were able to get into the business
before their company cared about DEI. That makes it hard for new people
to work up the ranks. While institutional history is valuable within an organization, it must also be recognized that seniority policies can entrench systemic biases within a company, undermining DEI and reducing the number
of diverse people who are able to be promoted to positions of increasing
responsibility and authority.

Expect Cultural Pushback

No matter how progressive the goals, or even how much support they gar-
ner at the top of the organization, the fact is, not everyone is going to
agree with an organization's goals. Not only that, but a segment of the
workplace population will not adopt these goals because the employees
feel threatened. To them, supporting the progress of others means they are
in danger of ensuring their own obsolescence. The fact that they are in the
majority matters little. Straight white men are not endangered in corporate
America, as evidenced by the fact that while the number of female CEOs in
Fortune 500 companies is on the rise, there were only forty-four of them as
of May 2022.[8] And yet a frequently quoted study by Ernst & Young that was
conducted in 2017 found that one-third of respondents said the corporate
focus on diversity had excluded white men, eliciting concerns about so-
called reverse discrimination and sparking resentment and anger.[9]

As Mills's theory on white ignorance reminds us,[10] a part of white culture
is to fight back against a narrative that acknowledges white privilege. Therefore it is to be expected that within almost any corporate culture, the white,
heteronormative, middle-class narrative, which is embraced as "normal,"
will perceive DEI as a threat to it. This attitude will dictate how quickly
DEI efforts gain traction and, more to the point, whether they will ever be
accepted. Therefore, planning for cultural pushback is critical to sustainable DEI work. Managers should not only anticipate such pushback (see the
Seven Stages in chapter 4) but also view it as retrenchment, not merely as
the company being risk averse or cautious for "legitimate" business reasons.

The Danger of CYA Culture

One of the biggest barriers to progress is the "cover your ass" culture, which is rampant in corporate America. It's classically defensive: every move is calculated to avoid loss and dodge blame, even at the expense of doing little or nothing. I heard an old adage recently that sums up this attitude perfectly: "If you do nothing, you can do nothing wrong." I did not learn what CYA culture was until I was in my forties. Within the world of organizing and community building that I had come from, the idea of covering your ass was not acceptable. Being accountable for your actions comes with the territory of leading change work; furthermore, losing on occasion—whether on a campaign, a policy vote, or a community initiative—is also part of the organizing culture. Therefore it's expected that people will gather themselves, take responsibility, and move on as a team. You cannot cover your ass and still catalyze change because change requires experimentation, and that implies occasional failure.

In the corporate context, CYA seems to happen not only with employees and managers but also with the consultants brought in to analyze a company's culture. For example, I am often amazed at how sanitized the questions in employee surveys are and how survey outcomes are contextualized. No wonder the results are so watered down as to yield little data worth using to make decisions! For example, I have seen employee surveys that generate 100 percent agreement on something, which immediately raises red flags. No issue ever results in complete agreement (other than, perhaps, "Are you a human being working for this company?"). Not even within the black community is there 100 percent support for DEI. Even responses in the high ninetieth percentile make me suspicious, and I begin indexing the responses. A high level of agreement tells me everyone knows how to answer the question, and it's nothing more than a CYA exercise—at all levels, from the person writing the survey questions to the employees answering them. No wonder such responses do not yield significant data worth exploring.

As an example, I worked with one client on a survey question that asked about enthusiasm for DEI in the culture. The results came back with some very low scores. Rather than accept that that's where it was as a company and the need to work on convincing white employees of the benefits of diversity, the company conducting the survey explained it by saying, "You have been doing such great education that people don't feel they need any more." This response is textbook white ignorance and does not help the company move from intention to impact. Where CYA culture is insidious—from the CEO to middle managers, front-line employees to consultants—it prevents everyone from taking risks. Innovation slows and culture becomes stagnant. Normalcy is valued over curiosity.

Banking while black is CYA behavior in bank branches where tellers, who are often among the lowest-paid employees, are personally liable for any error that occurs in their bank drawer. Therefore, these tellers are more interested in preventing any error that could cost them personally than they are in providing excellent, equitable service. The example in chapter 5, when Ryan Coogler was questioned by police after trying to withdraw $12,000 from his own account, illustrates this perfectly. The bank teller, who was black, knew she would be liable if this turned out to be a scam. Rather than take any action, she went to her manager, a white woman, and together they decided to call the police on the grounds of suspicious activity. Viewed through this lens, there was no other potential outcome to this incident because the teller and the manager were motivated by CYA—specifically, protecting their jobs and financial well-being. As a result, they exposed the bank to reputational risk, and all because they did not have the agency to act on their own. In this type of culture, CYA behavior is the best way to get ahead.

To respond to and prevent such incidents, our firm's Dignified Banking Training module calls out this responsibility placed on tellers, who otherwise have very little power. They have no incentive to speak up or speak out; all they are motivated to do is protect themselves against bad transactions. In light of what they earn, it makes perfect sense that they default to saying no to any request that is remotely out of the ordinary.

The takeaway for any business in any industry is the following: there may be similar procedures in your customer service that reinforce a CYA culture and end up becoming sticking points. This is completely counterproductive for DEI, which requires employees and middle managers to take chances, challenge assumptions, and embrace new and different ideas. People need to be open, not afraid, and willing to stretch themselves in unfamiliar ways so they can learn, which means they will make mistakes. While killing CYA culture is healthy for any company, it is essential for DEI to make an impact. And for that to happen, DEI structure must report to the

CEO so that it does not get bogged down in hierarchy and CYA behaviors that can derail it.

Candor and vulnerability also must be encouraged and valued to put an end to CYA culture. Top leaders need to model it, willingly and publicly challenging their own long-held ideas and admitting to the necessity of real and sustainable change. And that will take new communication paradigms, anchored in curiosity. As Larry Fink, CEO of BlackRock, said in a statement issued after the George Floyd murder, "We can only heal these wounds—building a more diverse and inclusive firm and contributing to a more just society—if we talk to each other and cultivate honest, open relationships and friendship."[11] For that aspirational statement to become reality, companies must get curious—including about whether their hierarchical cultures encourage employees to stay silent, go with the flow, and avoid getting in trouble.

Culture Audits and What They Uncover

A culture audit allows organizations and their departments to identify what I call the "stuck places"—those elements of business culture that pose barriers to DEI goals. Without a systematic assessment and identification process, it is nearly impossible to overcome and transform the existing business culture—or to transcend the barriers in America's culture.

When a DEI culture audit is undertaken, all the forces and elements that shape a culture are unearthed and examined. The process dissects the organization's culture with the goal of identifying barriers to implementing a DEI strategy. Just as important, the audit should uncover the strengths within a culture that can further DEI. These cultural strengths, such as collaborative teams, robust training, and a healthy communication infrastructure, are the tools to use. Typically, there is a mix of positive and negative elements.

Based on the many culture audits our firm has conducted, some of the more common findings include attitudes, written and unwritten practices, conscious and unconscious biases, and beliefs about "how things get done" that define the culture more tangibly than all the mission and vision statements combined. Until these factors are unearthed and addressed, real progress on DEI will not be possible. Below are several of the attitudes and assumptions that we have encountered in culture audits with our clients.

• Seeing DEI as Charity

When a company commits to DEI, one of the most common questions, as we have discussed, is, "Are we going to hire less-qualified people in order to be diverse?" This question is not only ignorant, it flies in the face of the data. DEI is not charity; it is a smart business choice.

Many people of color within an organization are overqualified for the positions they hold because of bias that keeps them from being promoted into positions of greater responsibility. Second, diverse teams build value and increase the profitability of companies by expanding viewpoints and perspectives and, as a result, becoming more innovative; in short, diversity has been proven to be good for business.[12] Therefore, the very question of qualification is steeped in white privilege and the assumption that there are no diverse candidates that could be better than the white employees who are already in the company. It's a great example of racial stupidity, as discussed in the first part of this book.

Another way that "diversity as charity" becomes part of the erroneous thinking in companies is when so much DEI work is funded by charitable foundations, not companies' own operations. When analyzing the pledges made after George Floyd's murder, we could see that so much of it came out of foundations and went to nonprofits. Tellingly, this separation does not allow for true equality in capitalism and instead reinforces white people having the power to bestow on people of color. Equity in capitalism means everybody gets a chance at ownership and wealth creation. So why not create the opportunity so that we all get to make money together?

• Saying You're Committed but Not Buying into the Steps It Takes to Change

Very few people will disagree with the statement that everyone deserves a fair shake. But when you actually start changing policy and tying DEI progress to budgets, the mood within a company shifts perceptibly. All of a sudden, fairness feels unfair, and now a breeding ground for conflict. Saying we are going to interview more women suddenly gets interpreted as women getting "special treatment," ignoring the special treatment men have had for centuries in the workplace. When someone is privileged, fairness feels like getting less. But that's only the perception as shifts happen within a company committing to greater fairness and balance.

• Resistant Middle Management

Once again, we come back to this central point: middle management is the oversized keeper of a company's culture. In our employee work, managers are the most common reasons people feel that they belong or don't belong at a company. It's not enough for the C-suite to care; middle managers have to, in both their words and actions. Regardless of what CEOs say at town halls, it's the middle managers and team managers who are the arbiters of company culture every day. They translate the culture, hold the careers of employees in their hands, and are some of the hungriest to get to the top, while often feeling the most betrayed. These are people who harbor thoughts such as having "dedicated their lives to a company just to be told they were passed over for a promotion by a woman."

Two effective solutions are DEI training for middle management and willingness to let go any middle managers who refuse to buy in. The bottom line is simple: if middle managers do not want to evolve the company culture, it will not evolve while they are still managers. When you as a leader find yourself in that situation, create a plan to replace resistant managers.

• The False Belief That Being a High Performer Makes You a Good Manager

The label "high performer" puts an emphasis on sales or profitability, but being a high earner for the company does not mean someone can manage a team of people and lead them to also become high performers. Individual success does not equate with good management. It's important to have emotional intelligence standards for managers and introduce them to the concept that it's not enough to make money for the company; managers must also contribute positively to a diverse work culture.

• Succession Plans That Do Little to Change the Status Quo

A function of good leadership for any company is ensuring quality leaders are developed, whether for the next few years or the next generation. Therefore, companies that commit to seeking diversity and promoting DEI need to look very closely at their succession plans to see how many open seats they realistically will have at the highest level. Then they need to ask themselves, who is being groomed to occupy these positions? If diverse talent is not identified early and groomed for advancement as part of succession planning, then very little will change within an organization's culture or its composition.

• No Budget, No Time

Show me your calendar and budget and I will tell you what you care about. Thinking you can solve your DEI problem without spending money is quixotic. Yet time and time again, companies will try to do just that: change their culture to become more inclusive without making an investment to do so. Just think how much money and time your company has spent creating the culture it has currently, spending on management programs, performance evaluations, bonuses, and even office space. It's important to be open to spending money and giving your company time to learn, practice, and create new cultural norms. However, just throwing money at the problem is a surefire way to fail, and uninformed action can be dangerous.

• Exhaustion of People of Color, Especially Black People

A company's commitment to DEI also must take into account that people of color, especially black people, are already tired from the daily experience of being an excluded class. When looking at DEI efforts for a company, it's important that there be a reparative element for the people of color who are already in your company. Such efforts should recognize what they have been navigating in the current work culture.

Mary-Frances Winters speaks to this phenomenon in her book *Black Fatigue: How Racism Erodes the Mind, Body, and Spirit*, documenting the science behind what she describes as the "fear, frustration, anguish, and, yes, rage that is a regular part of many Black people's daily lives and how it affects the mind, body and spirit."[13] Such emotional fatigue makes it hard for black people to extend the generosity of interpretation to any DEI effort. Instead, what's usually seen is a wait-and-see approach, which can be wrongly interpreted as negativity and lack of action.

In looking at this list of internal roadblocks and gatekeepers that undermine effective DEI implementation, the prospect of changing culture may seem daunting. However, the good news from companies is that these challenges can be overcome, if they are planned for and mitigated. While that may feel overwhelming at times, as if your company needs a complete overhaul, take comfort in the fact that you don't have to change everything for everything to change. For starters, shifting the culture toward curiosity helps lubricate the gears to put other change into motion. The healthiest cultures are the ones that are curious and open to outside ideas and people. Creating a culture that is curious about inclusion paves the way for meaningful change.

Building a Curious Culture Starts with Building Organizational Empathy

Curiosity and empathy act in tandem. Empathy is crucial to creating a culture that shifts from being concerned about change to being curious, and curiosity also builds empathy.

The types of empathy needed in a company's culture are best defined by the work of Clark, Robertson, and Young on organizational empathy, "I Feel Your Pain," which discusses cognitive empathy seeking to intellectually understand others and their internal states.[14] This response can be found when we hear that black people are killed by police at more than three times the rate of white people. Such data can trigger cognitive empathy to help people understand the plight of the excluded. Affective empathy means to feel and understand another person's emotional state. An intensely emotional example is how most of us felt when we watched George Floyd being killed on video for nine minutes. Hearing him call for his mother, saying he could not breathe, made it hard even for white people to avoid feeling the horrific nature of his death.

The 3 L's: Best Practices for Building an Empathic Culture

After the murder of George Floyd, our firm was inundated with calls from well-intentioned white people wanting to know the best way to respond. In response, we codified the 3 L's: listen, learn, and love. Through our 3 L training, we could help white people learn what to do and respond in ways that the black community has been demanding for more than four hundred years. Similarly, embedding these processes in company culture will help anyone learn more about how to engage with diverse people.

- *Listen:* This is the catchup work or the prework. People must engage in this on their own in order to develop at least some situational awareness. There is a treasure trove of content created by BIPOC communities to help any audience better understand what people of color are feeling and asking for. For some, it might be too much, as seen in the fight to ban the teaching of honest history in schools. However, listening allows people to just absorb the last four hundred years of content and better understand where different communities are coming from. For example, many companies put Juneteenth as a holiday on the corporate calendar after George Floyd's murder. While it was nice, it was nowhere on the list of things black people were asking for—like criminal justice reform. Declaring this day a holiday made the effort feel like assuaging guilt rather than making culture more equitable.

Listening also helps people avoid faux pas in speaking and interacting with others. They understand who the authentic leaders are for a community. I always tell my clients there are black leaders whom black people follow and then there are black people whom white people talk about. Often these are not the same people. It's important to know the difference, and listening to the community will help clarify the difference. In addition, there is an important way to listen so that it leads to an open mind. My dear friend Susanne Goldstein, who coaches women leaders, talks about it as "listening to be changed." Most people, however, listen to be confirmed, rather than listen to learn something new, making it no surprise that confirmation bias is one of the most prevalent of all biases.

To institutionalize listening, organizations should offer a library of relevant texts from the communities they want to include. Use cultural heritage months as a time to bring in authentic voices from diverse communities. For example, we have several clients using our firm's cultural calendar as a fun and safe way to explore what other people celebrate and the traditions they hold dear.

Listening helps people learn the norms and social mores so that they can catch up on DEI without stumbling out of the gate. For example, if Starbucks had listened before the company decided to launch its "Race Together" campaign, meant to stimulate conversation, it would have known that just talking about race without a justice point of view is white privilege all over again and would not be well received by any community. Indeed, the company's campaign was met with widespread criticism and even outrage.[15]

- *Learn:* Once people have spent some time listening, they have prepared themselves to learn in a respectful and informed way. They can begin to interact with communities to learn in real time how to be an ally. Rather than asking people of color to respond to your plan, find out how *you* can support *their* plan. People can learn wrong things, so understanding what the actual community says helps establish a basis for where and how to learn. *So what should you learn? How you can be in the right relationship with the community?* This starts with observing without judgment. To decenter the white narrative, one must first learn about the narratives of BIPOC people who are invisible to the mainstream and engage in a way that builds empathy instead of placing the burden once again on people of color.

I was at a summit meeting convened to help people in power meet those who need their help to build equity. Meetings like this often make me nervous because the very premise for the meeting reinforces whiteness and its power. And, as is so often the case, when white people in power decide something is helpful and a good idea, that's what matters. The opening night of this summit was meant to help white people understand the BIPOC experience by having a select group of people of color talk about racist episodes in their lives, such as being pulled over by the cops and searched. Some of the panelists were brought to tears remembering these horrific experiences. Asking BIPOC people to share and reshare their traumas is not how you learn about their lives or how to help. If the attendees really wanted to learn about racism in a predominantly white space, bringing in a white ally expert would have helped them reduce their ignorance without retriggering BIPOC people.

Good learning looks like assuming the person you are learning from has something to teach you. A learning example in my own life happened when I was working with the disability community. I could learn a lot from hearing panels, but not as much as I learned from supporting the disability community in navigating this inaccessible world. Donald Washington, a disability activist who started Missing Pieces, a project for the autistic community, said it best when he told me, "Don't pity me; respect what it takes me to navigate your world." Good learning looks like discovering and respecting what people have to do to make it through a majority-centered world.

- *Love:* Taking loving action ensures that the work organizations are doing will be well received and relevant to the communities they hope to include. It builds generosity of interpretation and will help every action be authentic, not hypocritical. When we talk about love, we immediately think of the Valentine's Day or Mother's Day kind of love. But a tenet of American culture is phileo, the Greek idea of friendship/team love, which is the cohesion within any group. Unfortunately, since the end of the Civil War, defining phileo to include other races has not been very successful, which is why it's important for company culture to transcend race. This helps ensure a "friendly love" shared among teams and employees. I witnessed this recently in a discovery group conducted virtually for a multinational company and attended by colleagues located in North America, Europe, and Asia. When the group dispersed into breakout sessions, a black employee in the United States was paired with a white colleague in Northern Europe to discuss their experiences at work. Afterward, when they reported back to the group what they had learned, the European colleague spoke with passion and visible emotion about discovering the bias and exclusion his discussion partner had endured—and his sincere desire to do something about it. As I told the group, "That's what allyship looks like."

To take a closer look at the 3 L's, and at loving action in particular, here is an example from one of our biggest client companies. State Street is a global bank with $3 trillion in assets under management and moves over 15 percent of the world's wealth. When George Floyd's murder shook the world, State Street knew it had to do something to respond.

In the immediate aftermath of Floyd's murder, Paul Francisco faced both personal trauma as a black man and the need to provide leadership as chief diversity officer of State Street Corporation. He had worked for years with the State Street board chair and CEO, Ron O'Hanley, and the two of them had established trust. Out of that conversation, O'Hanley decided he wanted to listen and learn first so that he could articulate a thoughtful response. "Instead of just making a statement, he wanted to have intention and actions behind his words," Francisco recalled.

One of the first actions taken was to convene a town hall–style meeting and "fireside chat" between O'Hanley and Francisco, with more than six thousand State Street colleagues participating live; later, a video of that conversation received more than 45,000 views. "It was just a conversation—no script," Francisco recalled.

As part of that meeting, he related a personal story of walking his dog through his neighborhood at nine o'clock one night when a police cruiser pulled up. Two policemen got out and approached Francisco, explaining that a neighbor had reported a "suspicious person" in the area and asking if he had seen anyone. During their interaction a white male, who was not familiar to Francisco as living in the neighborhood, walked by in the other direction, and the police didn't even look his way. That's when he knew exactly what was going on. He said to the cops, "I live around the corner. I'm out here, walking my dog. So, am I the suspicious person?" The policemen backed two steps away, trying to assure him, "Oh, no, no."

"It told me, once again, that it doesn't matter how successful you are as a black person in America, you are still put under heavy scrutiny," Francisco said. "I wanted my white colleagues to understand that what they experience is not the same as what people of color experience every day."

This chat modeled a way for State Street employees to listen and learn about racism without taxing the BIPOC community. It was also a powerful example of what we at Lazu Group call the 3 L's in action—listen, learn, and love.

As CEO, O'Hanley followed the 3 L's when he stated on that town hall meeting that he intended to take the next few weeks to listen to employees, learn all he could, and then decide what the firm would do as its response. He also encouraged employees to do the same.

Out of that listening and learning campaign, State Street put in place its "10 Actions to Address Racism and Inequality." Listed on its website, the actions commit State Street to specific goals and to be publicly accountable for achieving them. They are:

1. Improve Black and Latinx employee representation.
2. Sharpen focus on Black and Latinx talent development.
3. Conduct anti-racism conversations and training.
4. Implement diversity, equity and inclusion (DEI) practices for management committees.
5. Increase spend with Black and Latinx suppliers.
6. Improve Black and Latinx board representation.
7. Leverage SSGA's (State Street Global Advisors') asset stewardship efforts.

8.   Improve Black and Latinx representation across our industry.

9.   Establish combatting racism as a priority for State Street.

10. Increase civic engagement and reflection.[16]

The 10 Actions touch every part of State Street's operations, from talent recruitment to supplier diversity, from philanthropic activities through its foundation to making a difference in the community and across society. To take these actions, State Street needed to look critically at its current policies and practices, from how people were appointed to executive committees to why the company recruited largely from Harvard University, Boston College, and MIT, but not from historically black colleges and universities that could help ensure the best, diverse talent on the team. It examined its values, as well as the language used to convey them—and did that globally, from region to region, where differences in specific practices may not always be congruent with policies.

"The 10 Actions are probably more alive now because people understand that they have to be maintained and sustained," Francisco said. "We continue to ask ourselves, 'How do we stay true to these ideas?' Even as there are other hateful tragedies, we continue to speak out and point back to the 10 Actions."

At the same time, there is no disguising the amount of work it takes to make the 10 Actions part of the State Street culture. As Francisco said, "You cannot pretend that you are going to do things differently if you have not first fixed the hardware that makes the company run—especially in a 230-year-old company where things obviously worked for a lot of people. It's hard because you are challenging power, influence, status, and decision-making. It's hard, but it's also necessary. You have to make sure you are not alienating people. You need them to be part of the work and part of the culture change."

As this example shows, embracing the 3 L's will help create a culture that is open to difference, curious about change, and loving toward others. But culture can take a long time to change, so how best to set up a sustainable shift in your company's culture without waiting for naysayers to retire? The fact is, as explored in part I of this book, American culture has already changed and created new norms for including others, from black people to LGBTQIA+. The secret to making this more widespread throughout organizations is to decentralize it.

Decentralizing DEI Gets You to a Cultural Tipping Point More Quickly—and Sustainably

When the power is held in one place, at the center or head, actions and decision-making are almost by definition slowed down. While that may make sense in some business strategy contexts, it is anathema to DEI, which permeates the entire organization and its culture.

A well-known decentralized structure is that of Alcoholics Anonymous (AA), which has changed the addictive behaviors of millions throughout the world and yet has never had a formal headquarters or CEO. It does not need a centralized entity to exist. Rather, AA is an open practice that simply takes two alcoholics committed to abstinence through a series of twelve steps and an established tradition of consistent meetings that become known through word of mouth and sponsors. Inspired by this example of participation and commitment, any organization can embed new cultural practices within the company, starting with those who want to be a part of it. This establishes the momentum needed to reach a tipping point for change.

For over a decade I have applied this theory to my work on the streets with young people to the boardrooms of publicly traded companies. As discussed in chapter 1, decentralizing DEI gets broader buy-in and allows an authentic voice to emerge. While corporations are and need to remain centralized, decentralized DEI work leads to greater ownership across the organization, making this work more democratic and leading to sustainable success at every level of the company. In our work, we suggest decentralizing DEI efforts to create champions and catalysts at all levels who are able to take action for change.

In their 2008 book, *The Starfish and the Spider: The Unstoppable Power of Leaderless Organizations*, Ori Brafman and Rod A. Beckstrom introduce decentralized structures using the beautifully simple metaphor of a starfish that can regenerate its entire body and continue to live on even when harmed.[17] In contrast, a spider will die if it loses its head. In the same way, starfish organizations are hard to dismantle because their leadership is not centralized but sits in the networks that create the ecosystem. Like the spider, the centralized organization lives and dies by its head. According to Brafman and Beckstrom, decentralized organizations stand on five legs:

1. *Circles*—nonhierarchical spaces that people can join in a meaningful way to contribute the best of their abilities. DEI committees and ERGs are examples of possible circles. Circles are the building blocks of belonging. Think about an AA meeting. No matter where in the world someone is, walking into an AA meeting will feel familiar. This is what you want for your ERG circles, DEI committees, town halls and other non-hierarchical spaces. To ensure there is limited hierarchy, do not list positions of people who are joining, keep ERG lists in alphabetical order and ensure corporate sponsors are supporters but not leading. Have members take turns creating agendas for the meeting, create social openings for deepening of relationships and ensure protection for all participants.

2. *Catalyst*—the person who serves to initiate the change but does not own it. I like to think of catalysts as organizers—the people who jumpstart the action. A trail blazer vs a torch bearer. For example, Ella Baker was a catalyst for the civil rights movement. In fact, many will say Baker was the midwife of Rev. Dr. Martin Luther King's civil rights movement. Born in 1903 in Virginia, the granddaughter of an enslaved woman, Baker was the valedictorian of her class at Shaw University and became a social activist. She worked with the NAACP, then helped King and the Southern Christian Leadership Conference, influencing their work in human rights and voting rights advocacy. Today the Ella Baker Center carries on her work in communities of color.[18] In corporate structures, the catalyst is usually a diversity chief or HR head, but that may not be the most authentic catalyst. Often HR is nervous to catalyze authentic change and ends up catalyzing checklists. The position doesn't matter when it comes to encouraging catalysts. Their passion does.

3. *Ideology*—the value structure of a company, which encompasses why people would want to work for a company. Organizations that have a strong commitment to DEI as part of their vision and mission espouse an ideology that has true impact. When starting Future Boston Alliance to address talent retention in Boston (as discussed in chapter 8), we put out a manifesto that went viral and helped us find the people who shared our ideology. Candidly, not all of Boston agreed with us and we weren't looking for everyone. Sharing our ideology on YouTube made our goals and definition of the problem clear. It was critical we didn't waste our time attracting people who thought Boston had nothing to change.

4. *Preexisting networks*—ecosystems of people who join together in committed relationships and shared ideology and experiences. Such groups include ERGs and corporate social responsibility departments that strive to achieve impact. I was speaking to a company a few months ago, and their DEI chief asked about how to win people over. While that question may seem logical it's actually unnecessary and centers power in ways that are not helpful. Start with your true believers. You don't need to bring the naysayers along; that will kill your effort. Instead start with the internal and external networks of people who are excited about these efforts. It's okay to be protective about your DEI initiatives—that shows you respect the barriers your effort will face.

5. *Champions*—the evangelists of the new idea. In the corporate world, champions are often C-suite executives or managers, but they may also be an evangelist in a department that creates models for the company as a whole. Champions and catalysts work together—they reinforce each other to create and sustain momentum. A powerful example is King, who served as champion to Baker's catalyst, as the evangelist of non-violence and civil rights. US presidents called King to talk about civil rights—he was a spokesperson for the movement. But he was not the head of the movement. In fact, it was largely because of the work of Baker and others in the field that these presidents knew to call him.

Changing culture is a process, long and tireless, but the reward is well worth the effort. Establishing a curious work culture provides the rich soil for organizations to grow healthy and profitable decentralized equity efforts.

8 It's Not Them, It's You

Equality is unfair. . . . What's the point of a man working hard all his life, trying to get someplace, if all he's gonna do is wind up equal?

—Archie Bunker

"Sounds like you've landed, Congrats."

New England Patriots coach and general manager Bill Belichick probably had no idea that when he sent this text, unfortunately to the wrong Brian, he would be exposing the hypocrisy of the National Football League's commitment to diversity and opening up the NFL to civil rights lawsuits.[1] But that's exactly what this text did. Belichick was hoping to congratulate Brian Daboll on securing the head coaching job with the Giants and instead reached Brian Flores, who was preparing for the Giants interview for the same position, scheduled for a few days hence.

This incident, uncovered as part of the discovery process in a lawsuit against the NFL, revealed alleged long-term biases in hiring practices. This lawsuit flew in the face of the NFL's much-celebrated Rooney rule to encourage diverse hiring slates for coaches. Belichick's textual faux pas confirmed what so many black people thought about any organization's or company's commitment to diverse hiring: they don't actually mean it. Imagine being Flores, preparing for an interview for a position that has already been filled. What would it feel like to get dressed and walk into that room, sit on the other side of the table, across from Giants management, while everyone pretends to be executing an equitable hiring process? This act of apparent deception and pretense is one of the reasons companies have trouble attracting, hiring and retaining diverse talent.

What's even more insulting is reading headlines about CEOs lamenting that they cannot find diverse talent. Wells Fargo CEO Charles Scharf felt the heat when he complained about not being able to identify talent to hire at the bank. In a memo made public by the news agency Reuters, Scharf said, "While it might sound like an excuse, the unfortunate reality is that there is a very limited pool of black talent to recruit from."[2] A few years later Wells Fargo was back in the news for having conducted fake interviews with people of color when hiring decisions had already been made.[3]

There is much to unpack about comments like this. It is an excuse, it is untrue, and it is tone-deaf. White ignorance continues to promote delusional thinking regarding the outcomes of white individuals' behavior and systems. As Charles Mills writes, "The white delusion of racial superiority insulated itself against refutation."[4]

The fact of the matter for Scharf is that he and his organization actually don't know black talent because their world is devoid of it, as evidenced by the statistic, cited earlier, that 75 percent of white people do not have one nonwhite friend. America's segregated culture makes it hard for even the most well-intentioned HR teams to tap into diverse ecosystems of talent. White people typically do not have a lot of opportunity to interact with people of color and therefore have a white-only lens that reinforces a lack of socialization and prevents them from seeing the unique value of people of color. Even when white and black colleagues work together, they often do not socialize outside the workplace, which creates a barrier between them.[5]

As a result, organizations cannot find and retain diverse talent because the people who make up the company are culturally segregated from the communities the company wants to include. The company or its white recruiters do not know how to find or attract diverse talent and do not make the effort to authentically encourage them to apply—even though it would take only a quick Google or Facebook search to find, for example, the National Society of Black Engineers. More recently, companies have been reaching out to the low-hanging fruit, such as historically black universities and black sororities or fraternities and professional groups, but they have not yet established authentic ties with these organizations, as we'll discuss later.

Once diverse candidates do apply, the company culture must unearth and acknowledge its biases and be able to show the ways it has embraced diversity. Otherwise the company will have devoted no more than lip service to DEI. A life sciences industry client of ours shared a story from before our time working together. The hiring manager described conducting a final interview with a candidate and walking through the office with him. Suddenly she realized that everyone in the office was white. As they walked past the cubicles and offices, she felt the need to explain away why the office seemed so white. "I just felt like with every introduction I was losing any chances of him coming on board," she told us. "Why would he want to work in an office like that?"

When she offered him the position, the candidate declined, claiming he had received another offer that was too good to pass up. Both that hiring manager and I wondered if that "better offer" wasn't just the pay but also the opportunity to work in a more diverse environment.

The Google Lawsuit

For years, Google has highlighted its commitment to a diverse workforce. In 2014, Google became one of the first tech companies to publicize its workforce's racial and gender makeup in an annual diversity report. A recent lawsuit filed against Google in California in early 2022, however, paints a very different picture. The suit alleges that the tech giant fosters a work environment that marginalizes black employees, denies advancement opportunities to people of color, and ignores sexual harassment claims, among other violations.[6]

April Curley, a former diversity recruiter hired by Google, filed the lawsuit against the company, saying that during her six-year stint she witnessed people of color, including herself, typecast and placed in positions with no upward mobility, or passed over altogether. As a tech recruiter, Curley brought in new talent from historically black colleges and universities. Despite having recruited hundreds of young black employees for Google, Curley's lawsuit states, her pay was reduced by $20,000 before she was fired during the pandemic. She further alleged that there was a systemic practice of racial bias, that black people were not "Googly" enough—meaning they did not fit the culture—and that her concerns were not addressed when she raised them with supervisors.

Another prominent black woman, Timnit Gebru, was pushed out of Google after advocating for increased diversity in the tech industry. Gebru was a lead researcher on Google's Ethical AI team and is one of the highest-profile black women in her field, known for her work uncovering racial bias in facial recognition systems.

When Curley's and Gebru's complaints about how the company handled racial and gender discrimination reached HR, they were both given the same advice: undergo mental health counseling or take medical leave. After the women departed from the firm, nine other current and former Google employees came forward to say they were treated the same way. They consulted HR after colleagues allegedly made comments about their skin color or black hair styles or asked if they were sexually interested in their teammates. They also contacted HR to report retaliation after protesting sexual harassment issues and advocating for raises for black employees to match those of white colleagues. Each time, HR allegedly recommended the employees seek therapy or take medical leave to address their mental health—despite their mental well-being having nothing to do with their complaints.[7] An additional twelve current and former Google employees confirmed that this is a common practice by Google's HR department and is experienced frequently by underrepresented employees.

For example, this treatment was also reported by Benjamin Cruz, a former instructional designer in Google's Cloud division, who was shocked when a colleague told them that their skin was much darker than she expected. (Cruz, who is Mexican American, uses the pronouns they/them.) After reporting the incident to HR in 2019, Cruz was told to "assume good intent." Unsatisfied, Cruz asked HR to look deeper into the incident, and an HR official said an investigation into the matter had been closed, Cruz said. After seeking help from HR again, Cruz was urged to take medical leave and tend to their mental health before moving to a new role in the company.[8]

What's perhaps most troubling and revealing about Google's behavior is the continuous pressure and blame placed on the person of color to adapt to or fix the situation, rather than on the white person or the company culture as a whole. It's one thing to hire a large selection of diverse candidates, but without the proper DEI support, creating an integrated culture is difficult. If companies choose to act this way while enacting similar DEI efforts, they should also expect the same level of conflict. As discussed in chapter 7, until culture is addressed at a fundamental level, the success of DEI efforts in organizations will be stymied.

Once organizations accept that diverse talent exists, if they still cannot attract and retain it, they need to ask themselves three questions:

- Do we know enough people of color to have a pipeline of diverse candidates?
- Does my company understand the benefits of diversity to our bottom line?
- Are we an attractive place to work for people of color? (This last question is hard to answer because how do you know what's attractive to people you cannot attract?)

Being able to hold a mirror up to your company's culture and look at the ways your company is unattractive to diverse talent helps you build a plan to change it.

Through the Lens of the "White Gaze"

One theory that can be helpful to organizations in assessing and shifting their thinking is the term "white gaze." Nobel Prize–winning author Toni Morrison brought white gaze to life after being criticized for not writing stories for white audiences—criticism she embraced. "Our lives have no meaning, no depth without the white gaze. And I have spent my entire writing life trying to make sure that the white gaze was not the dominant one in any of my books," Morrison said.[9] In writing about the black experience, Morrison did not feel the need to explain black nomenclature or center the white experience. Rather, she centered on and loved black people in her writing unapologetically, and expected white readers to do their homework if they didn't understand. It was an invitation into black culture, not an expression of white culture in blackface.

In the work environment, white gaze, or centering the white experience to attract and retain white people, describes the constant pressure for people of color in America to center whiteness when presenting themselves or their work. Understanding this concept provides a context for hiring managers in understanding the effect on people of color and whether they feel safe in bringing their whole selves to their job. Expecting diverse employees to conform to the white gaze contributes to a company's retention problems.

White gaze also runs counter to authentic DEI work and the reality of the groundswell of calls for greater visibility of American experiences of the emerging majority. This is why it's important to begin establishing a new culture that does not need to center a white narrative and culture before inviting others in. In other words, you need to reflect on what is currently uninviting about your culture, which will give you the time and insight to build with intention toward impact and get it right, rather than just getting it done.

Get an Invite to the Right Parties

I have a favorite saying: "While everyone is invited to the DEI barbecue, people do notice how late you show up." Companies willing to take on the uncomfortable work of antiracism will reap the rewards of having been first movers. To do that, companies need to expand their networks or else diverse people will not bother applying for jobs because they think it's a waste of time.

The advice for leaders here is that, rather than wringing their hands, they need to work to retain their current talent and leverage existing community ties. This is an appropriate place for corporate foundation input, to help connect with relevant networks for diverse hiring prospects. It's important to create a strategy that has a chance to succeed in the new emerging culture. Recruiters are only a part of the answer. Company leaders, managers at all levels, and even the board need to do the hard work of building a pipeline.

Building a strategy to create a hiring pipeline starts with understanding what you are hiring for. Realistically, most open positions are entry level, but by looking at succession and retirements, you can also begin to understand what roles you will be hiring for in the next two to ten years. Creating a matrix of positions with leadership potential within the company and determining the hiring criteria (through a fair lens) will allow you to see what's possible. It will also reveal how much opportunity you actually have to move the needle in the short term. While not perfect, this will allow you to set honest goals rather than impossible ones.

The community aspect of the process needs to start with clearly identifying relevant communities. In other words, saying you want to hire more black or LGBTQIA+ people will never move beyond a declared intention unless you specifically address roles you want and need to fill. For example, if you need to hire more scientists, then you need to identify groups that can help you reach out to black scientists or LGBTQIA+ scientists. Find their ecosystems because—trust me—they exist. Building communities within industries is common practice. Once you identify the community, it is important that your company do its homework and research these organizations. It's not enough to know that the National Association of Black Physicists or the National Society of Hispanic Physicists exists. You also need to know the history, goals, and priorities of such groups.

A few questions to ask yourself during this process are: What organizations do we already support, and are they led by diverse leaders? Are these organizations national chapters or local? Is our relationship transactional?

Hopefully you already have some relationships within the communities you are trying to reach, which will allow you to create an asset map of your current relationships. These resources can now be included in your work of diversifying talent. Be aware, however, that any time you ask excluded communities to support your DEI efforts, that organization or expert should be compensated. Therefore, it's essential to know what your budget for community outreach is so that you can determine how many people you can respectfully include in your network.

Moving from intention to impact takes an internal honesty not often encouraged in corporate culture. Expanding your network requires candor in how best to make this outreach. You cannot say, "We want to get to know your organization because we don't know any black scientists. So maybe we can hang out and then send you some job descriptions." (Well, you could say it, but it won't help you build a pipeline.)

The best way to reach out is to practice the 3 L's—listen, learn, act with love. Because the harder truth to face and convey is: "We cannot keep ignoring black scientists and making them invisible. Because of our internal biases, we have ignored the black scientist ecosystem. How can we support your success through our business? We have also noticed your scholarship fund and the internship program you have created. We have signed up to support both. We think there's more we can do together."

Lead with your give, not your get. I liken this to when I was growing up and was taught never to show up to someone's house without a gift. I shouldn't expect to eat people's food without bringing something. Yet so many corporate relationships have the undercurrent of showing up without a gift. Corporations think their very involvement is the gift, but an invitation to work every day in a company that is fraught with bias is not as attractive as some may think.

The 3 L's can help you figure out how to introduce yourself in a respectful manner to the communities you are trying to attract. Taking loving action from the start (after having listened and learned on your own) helps communities recognize that you understand the history you are trying to overcome and are open to doing the extra work it takes to actually be equitable.

Provide your hiring managers with a toolkit that offers ways to reduce bias in interviews and the list of networks they can tap into, along with the recruiters, who should also be vetted for their diverse relationships. It's a cultural sign of belonging.

3 L's to being in right relationship

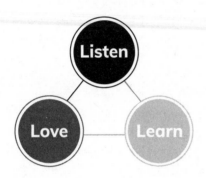

Listen: Seek out conversations about race, history, and the experiences of people of color on your own.

Learn: Commit to learning more about institutional and systemic bias to address and correct underlying problems within organizations and across communities.

Love: Take loving, informed action that is responsive to what you learned from the community.

Changing the Diversity Reputation in Banking

KeyBank has made a notable commitment to changing the banking industry's reputation when it comes to diversity. Those efforts earned KeyBank twenty-third place on DiversityInc's 2021 "Top 50 companies for Diversity" list,[10] one of several awards received in recognition of its DEI efforts. Importantly, this isn't just a superficial program. This effort runs deep in both company culture and business strategy, and from the top down.

Culturally, KeyBank has purposely sought to promote acceptance and valuing of employees' differences and viewpoints. For example, all employees are encouraged to join key business impact and networking groups (KBINGs), which function much like ERGs. The groups form around shared culture and heritage, including African, Asian, Hispanic-Latinx, Jewish, women, military, young professionals, and more. KeyBank credits the KBINGs with helping identify top talent, improving business innovation and development, developing professional and leadership skills, and enhancing the depth and breadth of employee and community relationships and networks.

Networking and recruiting on college campuses, employee referrals, and internal promotions are all strategies that have helped KeyBank become a more diverse and inclusive workplace. Beyond hiring diverse entry-level employees, KeyBank has tackled another challenge that often derails meaningful DEI work in financial services and across corporate America: ensuring upward mobility. This includes offering mentorship to young professionals who previously did not have access to it and an internship program that facilitates hiring diverse talent. Such efforts extend through all levels of the organization, perhaps most evident in KeyBank's having had the first and only female CEO of a top-twenty bank.

While the diversity award recognition has earned kudos for KeyBank, how the company functions day to day is the true reward for all who work there. There is a clear reason why KeyBank has seen so much success with its efforts: they run deep. DEI that seeks to check the box or hire diverse talent only at lower levels will fall short of the potential of creating a truly inclusive organization.

Attracting Diverse Talent

After four hundred years of legal and cultural segregation, overcoming the workforce gap and creating meaningful diversity and inclusion are not easy. It's hard to make up for years of ignoring a community by trying now to create diverse talent pipelines, especially in this environment of virtual working and networking. Many companies strive to achieve this by working with recruiters. However, it's important to work with recruiters who have a diverse slate from the top to the bottom. After all, if they can't do it for their company, they can't really help with yours.

Doing the due diligence will ensure you engage with a firm that actually knows people and how to be culturally competent, including how to look at applied skills and how to support candidates navigating the bias in your hiring processes. These recruiters have the expertise to introduce the candidates into your pipeline through meetings and events. You will want to know more about their hands-on approach, as well as a list of organizations and ecosystems they plan to include in the outreach. For example, are these organizations connected to your industry or rooted deeply enough in the communities to actually find people?

At the same time, you will need to examine the changes you are making in your systems through your cultural work to avoid reinforcing biases in hiring. Recruiting and hiring processes need to change. My focus here is discussing how to welcome new people when hires are made and introduce them to the community. Most corporate employee orientation programs have some component of DEI and commitment to equity. That's a great start, but there are other ways to make sure your employees of color are empowered and understand their agency to help make the company more inviting. For example, budgets for ERGs need to include spending on welcome processes for relevant employees, such as having a buddy system and making middle management introductions, all of which are key to helping people feel welcomed. People need to make time to build relationships with employees and help them know your culture. Convey to them that you understand they may be feeling like outsiders and that you are willing to change that perception.

Hiring is one piece of the solution, but it's equally important to have a plan to retain the talent you have. There is nothing worse than training your workforce only to have workers leave for your competitors. But that is exactly what happens when a company embarks on a diversity hiring campaign and then, in a few years, has to do it all again. This is yet another reason why thinking about your culture becomes imperative for any hiring and retention strategy you hope to implement.

Retaining Talent—in a Company and a City

When working with Greg Selkoe while he was CEO of the online fashion brand Karmaloop, based in Boston, we identified talent retention as a huge problem for him. He would hire from diverse communities, and within two years they would move to New York City or Los Angeles to pursue their dreams of expanding their careers in fashion. Time and again, these departing employees would say that they loved working for the company but hated living in Boston. Our solution? We created a talent retention strategy that included no less than changing the City of Boston. And so the Future Boston Alliance was born, initially funded by Selkoe, and I took the reins as the director.

It allowed us to create a movement that led to piloting and changing Boston's cultural problem. Where did we start? With what mattered most to the talent our city needed to attract and retain. That's why, when testifying at a talent retention hearing we held with the Cities of Boston and Cambridge together, we declared our desire for more diverse nightlife and the ability to take the train home after midnight. The issues resonated, as the *Boston Globe* wrote in a 2012 lifestyles article about the Future Boston Alliance: "They are familiar issues that have been bandied about for decades: What can Boston do to stem its post-collegiate brain drain? Why won't the city allow nightclubs to stay open later than 2 a.m.? Is there any way for the financially troubled T [the nickname for the rapid transit system] to continue operating past 12:30 a.m.?"[11] The alliance's other goals included increasing taxi service, providing more liquor licenses in the city, and permitting late-night hours for gyms and restaurants, all actions meant to make Boston more vibrant. But that also meant taking on everything from city regulations to the city's power structure, which won us some friends and supporters and some detractors. As the *Globe* also noted, "The loquacious Selkoe . . . and Lazu have become lightning rods as they call for change in a city that they say is generally an unappealing place for creative young professionals to live."[12]

Wins included the launch of a pilot late-night train service on the Massachusetts Bay Transit Authority (MBTA) system, inaugurated with an "MBTA bar crawl, from Savin Hill to Harvard Square," which not only promoted fun and entertainment but also allowed participants to experience different venues in the city. A shift in the mayor's office came about after an election in which culture was a campaign talking point. As the city began granting new liquor licenses, the alliance pushed for greater representation of people of color among the license holders, from three to nine (out of 1,900, so there's still a lot of work to be done in Boston). Nonetheless, our efforts were hailed in the Boston media: "No watchdog group has paid closer attention to the new licenses than has Future Boston Alliance."[13]

Local company employees loved to support these activities because they benefited from a sense of purpose and hope for change. These programs also allowed me to build an accelerator program for retail businesses that has led to thirty minority business enterprises getting to market, some of which became critically acclaimed and are growing, such as Boston While Black and Fresh Food Generation.

Future Boston Alliance disbanded in 2016. For me and so many other Boston entrepreneurs, artists, restaurant and bar owners, and others, however, the alliance's legacy remains: how to do grassroots activism within the business community. The legacy of this work includes a new narrative for Boston, one that the last two female mayors of color have adopted, including Mayor Michelle Wu, who appointed a cultural and late-night czar for the city to take up these very issues. For businesses and industries across the economy, this is also an example of applying the 3 L's and of how businesses can take a cultural approach to problems that feel too big to change. (As for Selkoe, he is still committed to attracting and retaining talent with his next investment, creating the most diverse gaming team in the country.)

The takeaway here is to make the retention strategy so embedded in your culture that everyone loves to be there and therefore doesn't even think about leaving. This is where you see a generational shift, with Gen-Zers and millennials willing to take a pay cut to work for a company that aligns with their values, whereas Gen-Xers and older generations rarely do.[14] The history we reviewed at the beginning of the book reminds us that the generations who grew up after 2008 question the capitalist narrative in a sincere way. They watched their parents work all their lives, only to lose their houses to foreclosure and their savings to medical bills; they don't see working as a guaranteed path to a stable life.

When striving to retain talent, it's important to look at the quality of life your employees want to have and help them achieve it. Equally important, if you want to retain talent, you have to work on giving others a sense of belonging. When people feel they belong, they are more invested in the organization. This means more than helping them reach their goals; rather, they entrust their work lives to you in return for a safe space for them to thrive. They need to know their value beyond your checked boxes and that you really understand the true value they bring to *business success*. They are the future of American capitalism that will keep you competitive.

Tips for Attracting and Retaining Diverse Talent

- *Start the minute you hire.* Your managers should understand how to motivate employees by being responsive to their needs and giving them opportunities to be themselves without judgment.
- *Get people into networks.* Making friends at work helps promote the feeling of belonging. ERGs, budgets for social events, and providing ways

for people to informally hang out and get to know one another are all important, especially for promoting team relationships and open communication.

- *Collect qualitative data to complement your quantitative data.* Integrate qualitative and quantitative data to get the most honest picture. It's time to jettison the "nine-box grid," a cookie-cutter employee assessment tool if there ever was one, that has been used by HR for years to identify and prioritize people who should be promoted and those who should leave the company. It literally pigeonholes people, from the "bad hires" with low potential and low performance to the "stars" with the highest potential and highest performance—but never takes in account corporate culture or managers' biases. While viewed for years as a tool for talent management and succession planning, it has the unintended consequence of imposing outdated, narrow criteria for who gets promoted. Diverse and underrepresented talent that has not had the same opportunities as white peers may not meet those criteria but have other strengths not captured in standard metrics.

- *Hire and promote diverse middle managers.* It's not enough to just have a couple of people of color or one black trans woman who checks all the boxes. Hiring and promoting more diverse middle managers will help DEI initiatives gain traction, promote performance, and attract even more valuable talent. A toxic culture, by contrast, can demotivate even the highest-potential diverse talent. As a consequence, without realizing it, companies may end up "managing out" the very people they need to keep. Instead, hiring and promoting practices need to intentionally open up opportunities for diverse talent with a broader set of skills, experiences, and perspectives, and who have much to bring to organizations and cultures that value them and their contribution. A place to start is by looking at what manager positions will open up soon. Concentrate on these first to hire and promote diverse managers.

- *Provide visible ladders to climb the hierarchy of your company.* Getting to the C-suite shouldn't seem like magic or winning the lottery to your employees of color. Having a clear plan for management is key, and it's also important to talk about what departments or roles lead to executive leadership and the C-suite. For example, a lot of diversity within companies sits in HR or public affairs. Yet it's very hard to become a CEO of a major company from HR or public affairs. Provide greater visibility and opportunity by establishing cross-department programs that allow people to see what different roles entail and what they need to do to get there. For example, when I first started working with banks, I was amazed by how many CEOs had started out as tellers. It wasn't until I got to know several of them that they admitted that they may have started there but they were quickly put on a management track. Some of them even had to be a teller for a period of time as part of a management program, so the narrative was not purely about CEOs working their way to the top from an entry-level position. That's why the ladders and programs for advancement need to be transparent. If people of color are not participating in them, engage with ERGs and other groups that can help you catalyze engagement.

The talent companies want is out there, and it's competent, motivated, innovative, and diverse. If that does not describe a company's current workforce, the problem is not with the labor pool or lack of candidates. The problem is within the company that lacks the culture to connect with diverse talent. In other words, it's not them. It really is you.

9   Vendor Procurement: Building Diverse Ecosystems

Coming together is a beginning, keeping together is progress. Working together is success.

—Henry Ford

Exelon Corporation, the largest utility company in the United States, serving more than ten million customers through six entities, is not necessarily associated with progressive thinking. An operator of nuclear and other power plants, it is the epitome of a large industrial firm. And yet Exelon made news in 2021 when it released its *Built to Thrive: Resilience through Partnerships—2020 EDBE Annual Report.*

The numbers it disclosed were eye-opening, but in a good way. From 2016 through 2020, Exelon spent a total of $11.2 billion with diverse-certified suppliers (vendors that have been certified by a third party to be at least 51 percent owned by people from a diverse background; often referred to as women- and minority-owned business enterprises, or WMBEs).[1] In 2020, alone, Exelon did $2.7 billion in business with diverse suppliers, for a total of $11.2 billion, which represents a 41 percent increase over the five-year period. In a statement, Bridget Reidy, executive vice president and COO of Exelon, said, "One of the best ways we can support diversity is to ensure that our dollars are spent with businesses that reflect the diversity we see in the communities we serve. We strive to apply these same ideals in everything we do, from how we build our workforce to the investments we make in nonprofit organizations across our service territories. It's not just the right thing to do, but it also makes us a better, stronger, and more responsive company."[2]

For Exelon, the increase in its spending across a diverse group of vendors and business partners has been a decade-long journey. Achieving recognition for its diverse business empowerment program entailed a lot of work, especially identifying and partnering with diverse suppliers. But make no mistake: this was a business decision. Exelon works with diverse suppliers because of the company's line of sight on innovation and customer service.

Robert Matthews, vice president and chief diversity, equity and inclusion officer at Exelon, explained the transformation of the company's supply chain process in a discussion at the MIT Sloan School of Management. The focus, he said, was on ensuring that diverse suppliers have equal access that allows them to compete for business with Exelon. Internally, senior leaders and other decision-makers are held accountable for supplier diversity. Externally, suppliers are expected to examine how they could work with diverse partners. "If we have a [supplier] company that can do the whole business, but we know that we are concerned about equity . . . how might we share that [business]?" Matthews added. Such partnerships allow large companies and smaller, diverse suppliers to work with Exelon and other major companies as well. This effort, Matthews added, is "really impacting the ecosystem so that capacity is being built in work they are doing for us and for others."[3]

Across the business landscape, vendor diversity is also a definable and measurable way to push back against social injustice. The lack of vendor diversity is a glaring example of how institutional exclusion has left out so many businesses, leading to the growing wealth divide.

As researchers have found, greater diversity in any company's supplier base helps promote socioeconomic agendas.[4] If businesses want to do more to show their commitment to DEI agendas, supplier diversity is one way to make an impact on a number of levels, socially and economically.

Stories such as Exelon's highlight that diversity in vendor procurement is achievable if companies are willing to navigate the transition. It's not rocket science, but it does take effort. Ideally, vendor diversity can help support the corporate cultural transformation. However, without the effort to transform the culture, vendor diversity initiatives will be next to impossible to implement and sustain. As the next logical step in the cultural transformation process, vendor diversity helps spread the benefits of greater diversity and inclusion across a broader ecosystem of suppliers, vendors, and partners. For example, corporate social responsibility (CSR) and environ-mental, social, and governance (ESG) ratings include a company's vendor diversity. Beyond that, diverse vendors can become ambassadors for a com-pany's commitment to underrepresented communities.

Over time, working with WMBEs is simply a part of doing business responsibly and ethically, to be a strong contributor to the economy and local community. But it takes more than just words; results matter most. As the saying goes, "No data without the story, and no story without the data."

Top Companies Lead the Way on Vendor Diversity

A 2021 report from consulting firm Bain and Company, with data from Coupa, which tracks business spend management, found that U.S. diverse supplier spending rose an average of 54 percent between 2017 and 2020.[5] Minority-owned business enterprises (MBEs), which account for a large part of diverse enterprises, make up 18 percent of all businesses, according to the U.S. Census Bureau data cited by Bain.[6]

The Bain report lists UPS, Target, and Pacific Gas and Electric Company as being among the companies that have been building more diverse sup-plier pools for decades, helping these companies improve business perfor-mance. Moreover, Bain refutes the assumption, held by many companies, that working with diverse suppliers could make them less efficient. Leading companies in supplier diversity have greater efficiencies in their systems that allow this business practice to take root. For example, according to the report, the top quartile of companies engaging with diverse suppliers have higher rates of preapproved spending (+10 percent), greater use of electronic purchase orders (+52 percent), faster requisition to order process-ing times (+18 percent), and faster invoice approvals (+46 percent) than their peers. Most telling of all, especially for longer-term efficiency, is that diverse suppliers have an annual retention rate that is 20 percent higher, on average, than their nondiverse counterparts.[7]

A significant takeaway is that vendor diversity should not be a stand-alone initiative. Rather, its greater impact comes from being integrated into the overall business.

An example is Target, which has not only increased its network of diverse suppliers but has also leveraged this network to expand the range of brands and products that it offers to appeal to more diverse consumers as well—clearly a business strategy that helps Target improve customer loyalty and its revenues. Target highlights its multicultural products, with black-, Latinx-, and Asian American–owned brands in beauty, skin care, and other products. It keeps an eye out for new opportunities and partnerships with programs such as "Target Takeoff," an accelerator program, and its Black-Owned Business Vendor Fair and LatinXpo.[8] Supplier diversity is not just within the stores; these efforts also involve general contractors for construction services, as well as technology support professionals.

As part of its overall commitment to supplier diversity, Target announced in 2021 that it plans to spend more than $2 billion with black-owned businesses by the end of 2025, including adding products across multiple categories from five hundred black-owned businesses. It also said it would increase its spending with black-owned companies in marketing, construction, facilities maintenance, and other areas. As Christine Hennington, executive vice president and chief growth officer at Target, said in a statement, "We have a rich history of working with diverse businesses, but there's more we can do to spark change across the retail industry, support the Black community and ensure Black guests feel welcomed and represented when they shop at Target."[9]

To keep enjoying such a reputation, Target needs to stand strong and consistent. Over the years, Target has enjoyed a reputation for supporting the LGBTQIA+ community. However, complaints and confrontations with employees in some stores led the retailer in May 2023 to pull some products and move Pride Month displays to the back of stores in certain locations in the South. In a statement, Target said, "Given these volatile circumstances, we are making adjustments to our plans, including removing items that have been at the center of the most significant confrontational behavior." In the next breath, though, Target also said it continued to support the LGBTQIA+ community and promised to be "standing with them as we celebrate Pride Month and throughout the year."[10] However, putting these displays in the back of the store—even if it's only one location—rewards bullies and reinforces feelings of exclusion. To be "in the back" is, by definition, to be excluded.

Going forward, eyes will be on Target to see if the retailer stands by its diversity commitments in terms of suppliers and merchandising, or if today's divisive political environment weakens its stance.

Moving the Needle on Vendor Diversity

Increasing vendor diversity is a process. As with every other aspect of improving DEI in the business world, it requires awareness, measurement, and willingness to change. With vendor diversity, the process starts at the logical beginning: assessing contracts that are coming up for bid or new spending in the budget. These new contracts should be prioritized. Second, break up the spend or budget dollars. Sometimes larger companies can handle vendor needs at scale but still take the time to investigate whether there are smaller companies that can do pieces of the work. If so, they should make the effort to include these smaller vendors in the overall spend.

As a matter of good business practice, it's important to pay minority vendors on time. This addresses a significant obstacle to doing business for many MBEs: accessing capital. As researchers have described in an article with the sobering title "'Why Even Bother Trying?' Examining Discouragement among Racial-Minority Entrepreneurs," getting financing is a discouragement for many minority owners.[11] Therefore, increasing their cash flow and economic viability with prompt payment helps these businesses immeasurably.

In our work with clients, we have identified several best practices for increasing vendor diversity:

- *Audit your spending.* Knowing where you are with your spending—how much you are currently spending, whether there is slack in the budget, what dollars are already committed but not yet spent, and so on—helps you understand your opportunities and potential for growth. It's also important to see what contracts are coming up for renewal and how much time you have to invite diverse competitive bids.

- *Make the business case.* As we have talked about at length in this book, DEI is a business imperative and having a culture that understands the business value of diversity will allow the organization to be more open to making changes. When you announce vendor goals, it's important to reinforce that, according to trusted business advisors such as Bain, this practice will positively affect the productivity and bottom line of the company.

- *Change the budget approval process.* Want everyone to meet their vendor numbers? Make diversity a part of the budget approval process. Set the expectation by letting managers see that those who have the most diverse spending get more money than those who do not diversify their vendors.

- *Be transparent with goals and progress.* One of the most effective ways to reach your goals is to show your work and make your data public. According to studies, some 85 percent of companies in the United States say they have dedicated supplier diversity programs. However, only about 59 percent of those with a program actually report how much they are spending on supplier diversity.[12] As more companies set the stage for greater transparency, it will help shape the definition of success, so it's best to be upfront and honest from the beginning. Vendor spends are so low that mere effort will result in increased numbers and a more authentic story to showcase your data. Being transparent also allows you to ask your community for help in areas where you may be struggling. Trust me, people will be more than happy to share names of WMBEs.

- *Audit your vending process.* Vendor processes can be prohibitive for many companies wishing to participate. Audit your payment terms to make sure you can be supportive of small businesses that need to be reimbursed for their outlays (e.g., on parts and supplies) and to pay their employees. Clawbacks, a practice by which money that has already been paid out must be returned under certain circumstances (sometimes with a penalty), can be particularly harmful. The $15 billion Big Dig in Massachusetts, which began in 1991, created a network of tunnels, highways, and elevated spans to reconnect neighborhoods. It was hailed as one of the biggest transportation projects since the railroads. While the project was fraught on many levels, as we've heard from the WMBE community, it was a tragedy for MBEs because of delayed payments and renegotiated terms. While the Big Dig is a long-ago memory for those driving in the tunnels under Boston, in the black community it remains a source of anger and contributes to distrust of development to this day.

  Start by diversifying your own budget. This will help you understand how your company will react to these changes and give you a good idea of your company's culture on this issue.

- *Practice participatory sourcing.* It's probably true that your company does not know the WMBEs needed to reach vendor spend goals; therefore it's important to create a participatory sourcing group. The group should comprise WMBE ecosystems that are relevant to your spend and managers high enough to approve deals with ESG/CSR targets. Get local and get specific. While reaching out to the National Black Chamber of Commerce is a great place to start, there may be local groups that are even more tuned in to the local business climate.

From Vendor Diversity to Industry Diversity

As companies increase their vendor diversity, they not only improve the economics and equity of their own business, they also contribute to greater diversity across their industry. After all, industries are composed of individual companies, and the more they expand their networks to include WMBEs, the more diverse and inclusive the industry becomes.

The commercial real estate industry has a reputation for being largely white and male.[13] This entrenched culture within the industry has posed a significant challenge to black professionals entering the industry. Among them are Gosder Cherilus, a former National Football League (NFL) player and founder and CEO of Bastion Companies. In a recent conversation with me, which I published in a monthly trade journal column I write, Cherilus explained his transition from a successful football career into commercial real estate, which he was first introduced to in high school and college through a series of jobs and internships.[14] He also knew that, when the time was right, he wanted to be a business owner and have a positive impact on the Boston community. As he found out, that was far easier said than done.

Cherilus explained: "I played football at the highest level, blocked some of the toughest defensive linemen in our league—but I was not ready for the fight that was ahead for me. I did all I could to get in, to network, and to learn the business. I was taking meeting after meeting to introduce myself and my company to literally every major developer in the city—and even the mayor's office, but never received a call back." Even legitimacy did not get Cherilus the visibility and callbacks he deserved.

After six years of trying to break into commercial real estate, Cherilus gave up and returned to football, joining a training camp with plans to get back into coaching. While at the training camp, he received a call from a Boston College classmate, John Hynes IV of Boston Global Investors, wanting to bring Cherilus into a development opportunity at Boston's Seaport.

Hynes convinced Cherilus to meet with him and his father, John Hynes III, at BGI—and that turned it around.

Today, Cherilus's Bastion is a venture partner with BGI on a project that broke ground in Boston's Seaport District, 10 World Trade. It's the largest project to date for him, for which he credits a bidding process that allowed every team "a fair fight for a bid." That process is the "Massport Model," a subcontractor and consultant selection model that deeply integrates diversity into development teams and projects.

As I wrote in my *Banker & Tradesman* column, this model did not emerge by chance. Rather, it resulted from the hard work and commitment of a group of black developers and others who leveraged their positions to get it done. Massachusetts state senator Linda Dorcena Forry first raised the idea. The model was championed by L. Duane Jackson, who served as vice chairman of Massachusetts Port Authority (Massport) and chaired its Real Estate and Strategic Initiatives Committee; Kenn Turner, a Massport executive who pushed hard for greater diversity in development projects; and Tom Glynn, who was Massport CEO at the time. Key support was also provided by Darryl Settles, developer and a founding board member of the Black Economic Council of Massachusetts. Thanks to their vision and commitment, the Massport Model became the standard across the industry, forcing developers to reach out and form joint ventures and other partnerships with WMBEs. When the Omni Boston Hotel, with black developer Richard Taylor, opened in October 2021 in Boston's Seaport District, it made history—and Boston made black history—because this was the first project in the Seaport that utilized the Massport Model.[15]

The Massport Model has been hailed as a significant DEI victory in real estate development, especially in Boston, which had long been called out for failing to move the needle on diversity. Traction, however, has been slow elsewhere. As the *Boston Globe* reported in 2021, the City of Boston spent $2.1 billion in contracts over five years, yet only 1.2 percent of that money went to black-owned and Latino-owned businesses.[16] In contemplating that sad statistic, Cherilus told me he believes there is an opportunity for more accountability and at scale, to continue increasing diversity and inclusion at every level.

For his part, Cherilus says he reaches out on every project to include more WMBEs and help them become qualified for projects by working closely with them. It's all anyone wants, he says: to be given a fair chance: "Having had the door shut in my face for many years, while knowing I was good enough to work on those projects, I became determined to create access and connect people to educate them more about the business. The future of this business is to expand and flourish with even more diverse ideas, greater equity, and the people willing to do the work to keep the gates open."

Diversity and Inclusion Leads to Community Building

There is so much good that businesses can do simply by doing better. Improving supplier diversity spreads the wealth of procurement spending to a wider variety of players, to help WMBEs—and develop a company's network. But it doesn't end there.

In addition, by increasing ties to the local community, companies can become a positive influence in the social fabric. We also see this in our work with commercial real estate developers, through inclusive development that strengthens their ties not only with residents, but also with businesses that could be tenants, partners, or neighbors. As a result, developers can win over "brand ambassadors" for their work. It's the heart and soul of inclusive development.

Within real estate development, inclusive development speaks to the social and economic fabric of local communities. For development to be inclusive, it must be authentic, transparent, and grounded in community engagement. In short, inclusive development gives the community a way to shape a project so it's relevant to them. At the same time, inclusive development helps developers meet their DEI goals in a sustainable way.

People in the community must see how this development will add value to their lives and their neighborhood, instead of just a checklist of what developers think communities like theirs need. Developers must be willing to bring in the community throughout the life cycle of a project, from planning to building and even after completion. This participatory development process allows developers and their teams to build authentic relationships with the communities in which they are working. As a result, developers and their teams can help shield themselves from costly mistakes such as permitting delays while building trust and momentum through each project phase.

The truth is that, too often, when development happens in a community, the first reaction is fear. The reason: development feels more exclusive than inclusive, as if it's meant for other people and not for the residents of the community. When development is done right, however, the opposite happens: people get excited. They see possibilities for themselves, their families and neighbors, and the broader community. Most important, they feel welcome in the new space. Inclusive development has the power to do all that, but it must start with trust. Trust is a two-way street. Developers must be authentically engaged with the community. It goes without saying that the plan being discussed must truly reflect the vision of what will be built. When developers ask for community input, feedback is considered meaningful and taken seriously. When that rapport exists, developers can trust that they're receiving 100 percent top-notch, accurate information from the community.

Finally, inclusive development is a great reputation builder. People will see what a developer wants to do and how that will empower the community with the kinds of spaces, services, and access that they truly need. More than that, the community will become a partner and an advocate for that development.

The result is not only influence on and within the local community but also impact—measurable and meaningful. Beyond commercial real estate, it's a lesson for other companies and industries to contemplate as a way to further their business strategies and their strategic agendas. The takeaway for other industries is the importance of developing DEI criteria that champion ownership and wealth creation. In real estate, the Massport Model isn't about hiring BIPOC janitors; it opens more doors for BIPOC architects and developers. In the same way, consumer brands and technology companies need to think about how vendors and suppliers compete for a share of their spend in a way that creates partnership.

Like diversity in hiring, vendor diversity will also deepen your relationship with BIPOC communities and build positive brand awareness within diverse communities. Vendor diversity can happen quickly if you are dedicated. Finding diverse vendors is not hard; getting your company to do it is where you will need to focus. Increasing competition is critical to a healthy economy and a core value of capitalism. The risk here is minimal, so lean in, save money, and get more personalized service. It's a winner all around. Increasing vendor diversity will innovate your company and the industry.

10 Where to from Here?

It's not where you start, it's where you end up.
—Zig Ziglar

Twenty years ago, when I was working with Harry Belafonte, he used to tell a story about Rev. Dr. Martin Luther King Jr. being asked if the black community was integrating into a burning house. "Yes," King replied, "and we must become firemen."

This story was vividly in my mind as I wrote this book because it's much the same for us now in the fight for DEI. Denial and aversion to taking an honest look at racism and white privilege, within corporate cultures and across society, continue to fan the flames of exclusion and systemic racism. Those fires were started by outdated and outmoded power structures, and people of color cannot be the only ones trying to extinguish them. Only if we *all* become firefighters can we unlock the trillions of dollars of economic value being lost to exclusion and bias.

Corporations have the independence and the power to achieve material change and move the needle on DEI. We see this in Exelon (discussed in chapter 9), showing us what companies can achieve when they prioritize inclusion. Ralph Lauren reveals the importance of taking action that is centered on the lived experience of their black and brown employees. These are two hopeful examples of companies that are doing the right thing around DEI—transforming their cultures and standing strong against the pushback that inevitably arises in moving from intention to impact. And they're not merely doing this work because it's the right thing or the nice thing to do. It makes complete business sense: it's what employees and customers are asking for—regardless of the Supreme Court's affirmative action ruling in 2023.

What makes DEI work so challenging and yet so powerful is its holistic nature. A shift in thinking in one place can spark renewal and healing in another. Corporate culture becomes a catalyst for social change. Experiences at work can have an impact on how we view our neighbors. We're all in this together, folks.

As Americans, we're connected through a shared, checkered history as a nation founded on the enslavement of people and stealing of land from and the genocide of Indigenous people. Only the unblinking admission of these traumatic truths can start us on the path of embracing diversity as our strongest strength. As we strive to remain a global economic power, diversity allows us to represent the globe. That, ultimately, is how we attract the workers—the thinkers and doers, the innovators and entrepreneurs—that this country needs. Denying the potential of DEI is biting off our nose to save our face.

By now in this book, you've read the business case for DEI—the journey from uncovering biases to doing something about them. You've learned what other companies are doing—or striving to do. It's time for you to ask yourself: Where do *you* go from here? This is not a rhetorical exercise; done right, it becomes a deeply emotional one. I've been in conference rooms, training sessions, and C-suite offices where leaders contemplating that question have wept. So here's what I would suggest:

- *Get curious.* Where has this book made you uncomfortable? Explore that. Where have you wanted to push back? Why is that? What is really stopping you from becoming a firefighter for America—and your own corporate culture?

- *Sit with your feelings.* Open yourself up to the emotions that may be swirling around and inside you. No condemnation is intended. But if you can identify what you are feeling instead of tamping down those emotions, you'll see more clearly what you want and need to do. Are you facing a daunting initiative that makes you want to push back? Are you prepared for friends and colleagues to disagree and resist your efforts? What will it take for you to find the courage to act, despite your feelings of discomfort and even fear?

- *Look at your ecosystem.* Are you part of the 75 percent that do not have any nonwhite friends? If you have children, are you exposing them to enough diversity? Are your children talking to you about issues that make you feel uncomfortable? Talk to your partner, closest friends, mentors, and members of your local church, book club, neighborhood group, or other communities in which you participate.

- *Create a community of practice.* Reach out to your peer ecosystem and create a safe space to explore DEI. Get to know executives of color and become familiar with coalitions of leaders of color. Among white peers, find those people who are genuinely on missions to become antiracist. Reach out to them, learn all you can, and encourage each other.

- *Adopt the 3 L's.* Listen, learn, take loving action. Make that your mantra as you seek to understand—and then use that understanding to inform your strategy. To reiterate what I've said before: uninformed action is costly. Those who are closest to the problem should also be close to the solution and should have the power. Adopting the 3 L's will help you develop relationships that make your strategies more effective.

- *Talk about it.* Where you work. Where you lead. Where you live. Where you socialize. Normalize your DEI efforts as business conversation. View it as the most potent breakthrough that can energize your workplace—jump-starting creativity, innovation, problem solving, and cohesion. Because it is.

- *Change your everyday actions.* What new habits and personal actions will help you become more inclusive? Start supporting minority-owned business enterprises. Holidays and special occasions are a great time to introduce MBEs to your family and friends. Fight for equity in your kids' schools or send your kids to a diverse school. As the saying goes, kids learn what they live.

- *Become antiracist.* Actively stand up for inclusion, equality, and justice. Don't just talk about it—be about it. This is the goal, as Ibram X. Kendi writes in *How to Be an Antiracist*: "Success. The dark road we fear. Where antiracist power and policy predominate. Where equal opportunities and thus outcome exist between the equal groups. Where people blame policy, not people, for societal problems. Where nearly everyone has more than they have today."[1]

- *Stay committed.* As you realize just how institutionalized racism is in your company, it's important to stay committed. Find an accountability buddy, someone who is ahead of you on this journey (just as the ideal gym buddy is the person who works out more than you do). If you don't feel safe with an accountability buddy from outside your organization, then choose someone on your board. To show the strength of your commitment, make it the basis of your bonus so that you will be judged by your actions.

What Allyship Looks Like

To be an ally or coconspirator, as it's more recently known, is to be deeply committed to change, even when that means giving up one's privilege. A powerful example is the life of civil rights lawyer Rita Schwerner, the wife of Michael Schwerner. She took a very public stance after her husband Michael, James Chaney, and Andrew Goodman were killed in 1964 by the Ku Klux Klan because of their civil rights work, especially helping black people of the community register to vote. (The movie, *Mississippi Burning*, was based on this heinous crime.)

As authorities balked at searching for the missing civil rights workers and local people dismissed their disappearance as a hoax, Rita Schwerner became the center of the news story as she demanded that they search for the three men. Rather than use her white privilege to find out only what had happened to her husband, she told the press that the family of James Chaney, who was black, deserved the same closure that she was seeking. As a young white widow, torn apart by her own grief, loss, and sense of injustice, she intentionally centered her message not on her own victimhood but rather on the numerous black people who face violence, death threats, and murder by white supremacy every day.

Later in her life she said in an interview, "I did have some sense that if the story was allowed to deteriorate into 'oh, this poor little white girl,' it would be offensive to everyone concerned."[2] Even as she mourned her husband, Rita Schwerner understood she still had privilege, and leveraged it to expand the spotlight to include those most affected by the actions of violent white supremacist organizations.

Allyship does come with short-term costs. Some white people will get mad that you are stirring things up, and excluded people will wonder if you're a fraud and whether you'll have staying power. Peers and colleagues will get upset that they can't hire the people they want. You will probably make mistakes publicly, and your company may even be the target of lawsuits. All the while your reputation is on the line as you expend your political capital.

Nonetheless, allyship will structurally transform your business, alter your leadership, and change you. This investment is worth it because it is nothing less than the profitable, sustainable future of corporate America and society. Along the way, though, it will come with challenges. Structural pushback to slow down the process will emerge, swift and subtle, seeking to undermine and even stop progress and hard work. People will distance themselves from you. When that happens, remember that Rev. Dr. Martin Luther King Jr. died a hated man, a fact that many today would like to forget. If you are not uncomfortable, you are not doing the work.

System changes do not happen overnight. They will not take root by only checking the boxes. Keep that in mind as you find ways to stay transparent, decentralize your DEI work, and resist CYA behavior. Show that there is another way to achieve equity in the workplace. Incentivize those who are willing to engage in the work. When you become tired and discouraged, find inspiration in the trailblazers of the past.

In 1925, A. Philip Randolph organized and led the Brotherhood of Sleeping Car Porters, the first successful black-led labor union. There's a story about him meeting with President Franklin Delano Roosevelt and first lady Eleanor Roosevelt in 1941, after Randolph threatened a protest in Washington against racial discrimination in the defense industries. Eleanor is credited with supporting Randolph and arranging the meeting with FDR at the White House. When Randolph stood up to Oval Office pressure to abandon the threatened protest march, FDR issued an executive order that created the Fair Employment Practices Commission to investigate and end racial discrimination in the defense and military industries.[3] As I learned more about this story, what struck me was not FDR's action in the face of Randolph's willingness to stand up to the president. Rather, it was a letter in George Washington University's online archive, from Randolph to Eleanor Roosevelt:

> Just a word in these days of crisis and of storm and stress to express my deep appreciation for the great service you are rendering in [your] own way to the cause of democracy in general, and justice for the Negro people in particular. I

need not tell you that there is a deep affection among the Negro people for you, because of your forthright and sincere advocacy in human justice.[4]

Who are the leaders of the movements who are being vilified today, who will become the heroes of tomorrow?

Even Joe Biden had to retract a lot of his political stances to win the presidential primaries in 2019, but he was smart to pick as his running mate Kamala Harris, the woman who called him out powerfully during the Democratic debates, declaring that his work with segregationist lawmakers in the past was "hurtful."[5] In choosing Harris—a woman of color—Biden made sure he made the right kind of history. Nominating and championing Supreme Court Justice Ketanji Brown Jackson not only fulfilled a campaign promise but also helped Biden solidify his political legacy.

Are you willing to do the right thing to be on the right side of history?

The New Entrepreneurs

A new type of entrepreneur is emerging on the business stage and knocking on your door. Young, diverse, and activist, these entrepreneurs are pursuing opportunity and catalyzing change. To elevate the new BIPOC majority in the United States, wealth and ownership need to be commensurate with the size of this population. Enter Known, cofounded by Nathalie Molina Niño, Ushir Shah, Jim Casselberry, and Valerie Red-Horse Mohl, who have launched a new financial platform designed to power the growth of the BIPOC-owned economy. The founders bring to this venture decades of investing, entrepreneurial, and fintech expertise. Their goal is to bring scalable solutions to closing the wealth gap.

Known's mission is to address the structural barriers in the financial system that keep BIPOC-owned businesses from growing to scale. Instead of waiting for financial institutions to get it right, Known is creating its own deals to responsibly drive capital and investment decisions to support the BIPOC economy, where too often ideas are ignored or not funded properly to ensure their success. This is exactly the kind of missed opportunity that leads to the economic losses that Citibank referred to in its $16 trillion estimate, as cited in previous chapters. In other words, Known is taking steps to close the wealth gap that the financial industry itself has helped create and perpetuate.

Because of their backgrounds, the founders know all too well how the "machine" works, with investors and institutions holding most of the power. As Molina Niño, who comes from a long career in tech, said in an interview, "And so that was the switch for me, when I went from being a participant and a founder and deciding: You know what? I'm going to stay in the business world, but I'm going to do it from another vantage point, because the investment world are really the group that's truly in charge here." As Known continues to gain traction, it will be interesting to see how its impact pressures the industry to take a hard look at itself.

Bea Dixon, a black woman and entrepreneur, launched the Honey Pot Company with a very personal sense of mission for plant-derived feminine care and hygiene products. As Dixon, CEO and cofounder, states on the Honey Pot website: "I was suffering from bacterial vaginosis for 8 months when an ancestor came to me in a dream and gifted me with a vision to heal myself. With her help I created The Honey Pot to solve for what other brands wouldn't through the power of herbs."[6] What started as a personal brand has gone big, being sold in Target, Walgreens, Walmart and other chains.

Her path to success has been charted through tackling taboos (ridiculous ones, I might add), such as getting investors comfortable hearing the word "vagina" as they would the name of any other body part. As Dixon said in an interview with *Glossy*, "I would always try to break the ice by saying, 'Look, we all came from a vagina. There's nothing weird about this shit. Everybody just calm down, we serve half of the planet.' My thing was always that I wanted to demystify this word. I wanted to take the sting off of it. I wanted to take the taboo away from it, and I wanted people to not feel shame if they had an odor, an itch, an infection, an STD or anything else. These are menstrual conditions and these are normal things that humanity deals with. It doesn't make it any better when [the word 'vagina'] is filled with trauma. I've always had that undertone because that is what sits at the foundation of what we do."[7]

Bold, confident, and not afraid to speak her truth—that's what this business world needs from a young female entrepreneur of color.

Gilbert Milam Jr.—otherwise known as Berner—is a rapper and successful entrepreneur who heads a cannabis empire known as Cookies—a brand that's worth an estimated $1 billion. As *Insider* described him, "Like Steve Jobs is to Apple and Elon Musk is to Tesla, such is Berner to Cookies; it's impossible to discuss the history of Cookies without him . . . [the] Bay Area rapper Berner, who also serves as CEO of the company that oversees everything from retail dispensaries to clothing design."[8] This is more than just weed; it's a lifestyle brand that is known for its clothing line. By leveraging street cred, his celebrity, and his entrepreneurism, Berner has grown his business rapidly, from zero to more than forty-five retail locations, including flagship stores in Los Angeles and San Francisco.

Even with all the success that Berner has amassed, he still sees it as his responsibility to ensure that others are included in—not excluded from—opportunity. Over the years, many black people have been arrested for their work in the prelegalization cannabis industry, and now the irony is that the legitimate cannabis industry is sometimes inaccessible to them. Berner is intent on trying to correct that. As he told *Forbes* in an interview, "I feel like it's our job at Cookies to empower some of the true players, some of the real [cannabis] breeders putting in the work, and some of the real brands that have been left behind. I feel an obligation to try to keep some of the key players in the game and bring them into the white market. I like to look at this huge platform as having a Johnny Appleseed effect by planting these genetics around the world. So, same game plan—just, you know, a little added pressure to make sure we bring the key people with us."[9]

I find in people like Molina Niño, Dixon, and Berner echoes of the stories of people in our history who worked to build models for change. This, above all else, gives me hope.

*   *   *

While I was writing this book, I had a first edition of *The Souls of Black Folk* by W. E. B. Du Bois on my desk. On an inside page is an inscription by Philip Payton, the Harlem real estate developer who was able to take an act of revenge between two white landlords and create a neighborhood that changed the world.

I think of Payton's dream to help build Harlem into a thriving community for black artists, business owners, and families. This movement brought us some of the twentieth century's most famous artists—Zora Neale Hurston, Langston Hughes, and Duke Ellington, just to name a few—who had a lasting impact on black identity.

Now, one hundred years after the Harlem Renaissance, we are still celebrating the movement that made Harlem a nexus for black culture, from

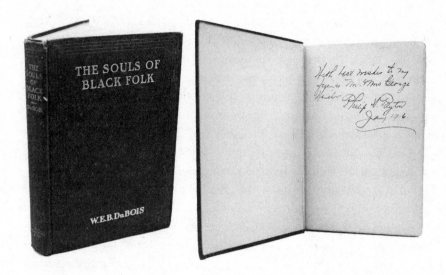

the organizing home of Malcolm X to the proving ground of streetwear kings like Dapper Dan. Harlem shows the benefit of diversity to the global culture and economy.

Reading Payton's inscription—"With best wishes to my friends, Mr. and Mrs. George Winslow Jan 1916"—I have to wonder what he would wish for us today. I can imagine him being excited by the lasting legacy of rapper and entrepreneur Nipsey Hussle. I can imagine him hosting the most amazing dinner to welcome Justice Jackson Brown to his Harlem.

Daydreams of the past may inspire, but a legacy continues only through the hard work of today. I am optimistic that we will choose to march toward justice because surviving by itself is not sufficient; we also want to thrive. But we will neither survive nor thrive if we do not stop and repair the racial oppression in this country. It's time to meet the moment and move the needle as much as we can and fight the social justice clawbacks that are sure to come. I see it every day in my work with businesses, from C-suite executives who pick up the charge to employees creating action-oriented ERGs.

I am optimistic because the numbers tell the same story. This country will be majority brown by 2030 and will be younger than it has been for years. Black and brown women are the most educated demographic in the country. Even though the racial construct is stupid, people don't have to be. I am optimistic because balance is what nature does. We'll find our equilibrium with race, which may be more natural than we think. After all, when you put children on the playground, they just play. In the same way, if we're just ourselves and practice the manners and love of neighbor that we were taught as children—and leave all the rest behind—we can find a way to listen, learn, and take loving action.

As I am writing this, young people continue to take to the streets to protest the ongoing epidemic of mass shootings. The Supreme Court ruling that overturned *Roe v. Wade* after fifty years has women and allies of all genders not only marching in protest but also developing ways for people to access safe abortions. Young people are here for change. The next generation has the baton now and as they run the next leg of the marathon they are intent on making change to save their planet and society.

The world is ready—and so, I hope, are you. As a leader, you have agency, no matter where you are in your company. Most important, if you are a manager, you have the confidence that will lead you further into leadership. You know your business, you know your company's culture, you know your colleagues and peers. Now it's time to leverage that knowledge and take action. Set a legacy that the next generation won't have to apologize for or explain away. Is corporate America genuinely interested in helping build equity? We will find out by how you lead.

Acknowledgments

This book is a reflection of both my life and my life's work. Countless people have helped, guided, challenged, and influenced me in my ongoing
quest to fight for equity, justice, and a sense of belonging. Among the many
I have encountered on this journey, I wish to thank my family, whose love
and support are why I am here. To my dear friends, thank you for always
taking the time to rearrange the world with me. Special shoutout to the
women who hold me down and keep me grounded.

To my mentors and champions, who teach, love, and encourage me.
Special shout-out to Richard Marotta, who gave me a chance to move levers
in business. Zebulon Vance Miletsky, thank you for talking me off the ledge
many times when I was writing this book.

Special thanks to the MIT Press for embracing the uniqueness of my
book, written as it is from the perspective of a lifelong activist who just happens to be deeply involved in the corporate world. I wish to thank Emily
Taber, who embraced this book from the beginning, and editors Catherine
Woods and Anne-Marie Bono, who helped bring it across the finish line. I
also want to acknowledge Patricia Crisafulli and Pat Commins, who supported me in researching, writing, and editing this book.

Last, by hardly least, to the clients, partners, and collaborators of The
Lazu Group: you make the work real and meaningful.

Notes

Introduction

1. Jacob Bobage, "Walmart Apologizes, Pulls 'Juneteenth Ice Cream' after Online Back-lash," *Washington Post*, May 24, 2022, https://www.washingtonpost.com/business /2022/05/24/walmart-juneteenth-ice-cream.

2. Daniel Wiessner, "Walmart Accused of Bias against Workers with Criminal His-tories," Reuters, July 20, 2021, https://www.reuters.com/legal/transactional/walmart -accused-bias-against-workers-with-criminal-histories-2021-07-20.

3. Henry Lewis Gates, "What Is Juneteenth?," *Bay State Banner*, June 10, 2021, https:// www.baystatebanner.com/2021/06/10/what-is-juneteenth-2.

4. Malia Lazu, "Going Corporate for a Cause," *Boston Globe*, May 31, 2019, https:// www.bostonglobe.com/ideas/2019/05/31/malia/j9o8nVbqh5bJqElWsFYZ3O/story .html.

5. The Gathering for Justice, "About," https://www.gatheringforjustice.org/about# tg4jstory.

6. Frederick Douglass, *Narrative of the Life of Frederick Douglass an American Slave* (Boston: Anti-Slavery Office, 1845), 32.

7. See the website of the Gathering for Justice, https://www.gatheringforjustice.org /six-principles-of-kingnian-non-violence.

8. Lazu, "Going Corporate for a Cause."

9. NPR, "Questlove's 'Summer of Soul' Brings Lost Music Back to Life," transcript, February 1, 2022, https://www.npr.org/transcripts/1075850442

10. Greta Thunberg, "At Davos We Will Tell World Leaders to Abandon the Fossil Fuel Economy," *Guardian*, January 10, 2020, https://amp.theguardian.com/comment isfree/2020/jan/10/greta-thunberg-davos-tycoons-fossil-fuels-dismantle-climate -crisis?__twitter_impression=true&fbclid=IwAR3qPblX2sIGfMMBLUsG2Kgp1Hjf7 mikD9W1uByfR7_H5F9GU-BPXuhmYyY.

11. Charles W. Mills, "White Ignorance," in *Race and Epistemologies of Ignorance*, ed. Shannon Sullivan and Nancy Tuana (Albany: State University of New York Press, 2007), 13–38.

12. Crystal M. Fleming, *How to Be Less Stupid about Race: On Race, White Supremacy, and the Racial Divide* (Boston: Beacon Press, 2019), 11.

13. Joseph Losavio, "What Racism Costs Us All," *IMF Finance & Development*, September 2020, https://www.imf.org/Publications/fandd/issues/2020/09/the-economic-cost-of-racism-losavio.

14. McKinsey Institute for Black Economic Mobility, "The Economic Impact of Closing the Racial Wealth Gap," 2019, https://www.mckinsey.com/industries/public-and-social-sector/our-insights/the-economic-impact-of-closing-the-racial-wealth-gap, 5.

15. McKinsey Institute for Black Economic Mobility, "The Economic Impact of Closing the Racial Wealth Gap," 6.

16. Losavio, "What Racism Costs Us All."

Chapter 1

1. Charles W. Mills, "White Ignorance," in *Race and Epistemologies of Ignorance*, ed. Shannon Sullivan and Nancy Tuana (Albany: State University of New York Press, 2007).

2. Zora Neale Hurston, "Quotable Quotes," https://www.goodreads.com/quotes/9580800-all-my-skinfolk-ain-t-kinfolk.

3. Barbara Clarke, "Write the Checks," LinkedIn post, July 11, 2019, https://www.linkedin.com/pulse/write-checks-barbara-clarke.

4. Stephanie Creary, Nancy Rothbard, Elena Mariscal, Olivia Moore, Jared Scruggs, and Natalia Villarmán, "Evidence-Based Solutions for Inclusion in the Workplace: Actions for Middle Managers," Wharton People Analytics, University of Pennsylvania, May 2020, https://wpa.wharton.upenn.edu/wp-content/uploads/2020/05/Evidence-Based-Solutions-for-Inclusion-in-the-Workplace_May-2020.pdf.

5. MIT Sloan School of Management, "The Inclusive Innovation Economy," September 28, 2021, https://www.youtube.com/watch?v=mXkTIBMrm0g&t=1722s.

Chapter 2

1. "Mr. Lincoln and Negro Equality," *New York Times*, December 28, 1860, https://www.nytimes.com/1860/12/28/archives/mr-lincoln-and-negro-equality.html.

2. Charles W. Mills, *Black Rights/White Wrongs: The Critique of Racial Liberalism* (New York: Oxford University Press, 2017), 41.

3. Mills, *Black Rights/White Wrongs*, 43.

4. Crystal M. Fleming, *How to Be Less Stupid about Race: On Race, White Supremacy, and the Racial Divide* (Boston: Beacon Press, 2019).

5. Connie Hassett-Walker, "The Racist Roots of American Policing: From Slave Patrols to Traffic Stops," *Chicago Reporter*, June 7, 2019, https://www.chicagoreporter .com/the-racist-roots-of-american-policing-from-slave-patrols-to-traffic-stops.

6. Tuskegee University Archives Repository, "Lynching Information," 2017–2022, http://archive.tuskegee.edu/repository/digital-collection/lynching-information.

7. Michael S. Rosenwald, "A Black Man Accused of Rape, a White Officer in the Klan, and a 1936 Lynching That Went Unpunished," *Washington Post*, July 19, 2020, https://www.washingtonpost.com/history/2020/07/19/atlanta-lynching-police-ku -klux-klan.

8. Tom Gjelten, "Peaceful Protesters Tear-Gassed to Clear Way for Trump Church Photo-Op," NPR, June 1, 2020, https://www.npr.org/2020/06/01/867532070/trumps -unannounced-church-visit-angers-church-officials.

9. Associated Press, "Obama Speaks Out as Nation Confronts Confluence of Crises," WBRZ, June 3, 2020, https://www.wbrz.com/news/obama-steps-out-as-nation-con fronts-confluence-of-crises.

10. Mills, *Black Rights/White Wrongs*, 19.

11. Dana M. Peterson and Catherine L. Mann, "Closing the Racial Inequality Gaps," Citigroup, September 2020, https://ir.citi.com/NvIUklHPilz14Hwd3oxqZBLMn1_XPq o5FrxsZD0x6hhil84ZxaxEuJUWmak51UHvYk75VKeHCMI%3D.

12. McKinsey & Company, *Diversity Wins: How Inclusion Matters*, 2020, https://www .mckinsey.com/~/media/mckinsey/featured%20insights/diversity%20and%20 inclusion/diversity%20wins%20how%20inclusion%20matters/diversity-wins -how-inclusion-matters-vf.pdf.

13. Jeroslyn Johnson, "The Longest-Tenured Black CEO among S&P 500 Compa-nies Steps Down at Carnival—the Number of Black CEOs Continues to Dwindle," Yahoo!, April 26, 2022, https://www.yahoo.com/video/longest-tenured-black-ceo -among-211554524.html.

14. Kiara Taylor, "America's Top Black CEOs," *Investopedia*, June 25, 2022, https:// www.investopedia.com/top-black-ceos-5220330.

15. Brandy Mabra, "We Need to Talk about Why We Still See CEOs as White Men (and How to Challenge That), *Fast Company*, March 22, 2022, https://www.fast

ਕkirimNaNOK

company.com/90732810/we-need-to-talk-about-why-we-still-see-ceos-as-white-men-and-how-to-challenge-that.

16. Anita Snow, "1 in 3 Fears Immigrants Influence US Elections: AP-NORC Poll," Associated Press, May 9, 2022, https://apnews.com/article/immigration-2022-midterm-elections-covid-health-media-2ebbd3849ca35ec76f0f91120639d9d4.

17. U.S. Census Bureau, *Population Projections* (Washington, DC: Census.gov, 2018).

18. Rachaell Davis, "New Study Shows Black Women Are among the Most Educated Group in the United States," *Essence*, October 27, 2020, https://www.essence.com/news/new-study-black-women-most-educated.

19. Cone Communications, *2017 Cone Communication CSR Study* (Boston: Cone Communications, 2017).

20. Tracy Jan, Jena McGregor, and Meghan Hoyer, "Corporate America's $50 Billion Promise," *Washington Post*, August 24, 2021, https://www.washingtonpost.com/business/interactive/2021/george-floyd-corporate-america-racial-justice.

21. David Smith, "Disney Faces Backlash over LGBTQ Controversy: 'It's Just Pure Nonsense,'" *Guardian*, March 21, 2022, https://www.theguardian.com/film/2022/mar/21/disney-faces-backlash-lgbtq-controversy-dont-say-gay-bill-florida.

22. Joe Hernandez, "Disney Workers Walk Out over the Company's Response to So-Called 'Don't Say Gay' Bill," NPR, March 22, 2022, https://www.npr.org/2022/03/22/1088048998/disney-walkout-dont-say-gay-bill.

23. Adam Smith, quoted in "Adam Smith on Slavery," May 15, 2019, https://www.adamsmithworks.org/documents/adam-smith-on-slavery.

24. McKinsey & Company, "Race in the Workplace: The Black Experience in the US Private Sector," February 21, 2021, https://www.mckinsey.com/featured-insights/diversity-and-inclusion/race-in-the-workplace-the-black-experience-in-the-us-private-sector.

25. UPI, "Reagan Civil Rights Policies Are Defended and Criticized," *New York Times*, May 30, 1983, https://www.nytimes.com/1983/05/30/us/reagan-civil-rights-policies-are-defended-and-criticized.html.

26. Deborah J. Vagins and Jesselyn McCurdy, *Cracks in The System: Twenty Years of the Unjust Federal Crack Cocaine Laws* (New York: ACLU, October 2006), i.

27. Kenneth Nunn, "Race, Crime and the Pool of Surplus Criminality: Or Why the 'War on Drugs' Was a 'War on Blacks,'" faculty paper, University of Florida Law Faculty Publications, 2002, https://scholarship.law.ufl.edu/cgi/viewcontent.cgi?article=1178&context=facultypub.

28. Erik Eckholm, "Recession Raises Poverty Rate to a 15 Year High," *New York Times*, September 16, 2010, https://www.nytimes.com/2010/09/17/us/17poverty.html.

29. Warren E. Buffett, "Stop Coddling the Super-Rich," *New York Times*, August 14, 2011, https://www.nytimes.com/2011/08/15/opinion/stop-coddling-the-super-rich.html.

30. Jon Meacham, "Show Them the Money," *Time*, October 12, 2011, https://ideas.time.com/2011/10/12/show-them-the-money.

31. Monica Anderson, Michael Barthel, Andrew Perrin, and Emily Vogels, "#Black-LivesMatter Surges on Twitter after George Floyd's Death," Pew Research Center, June 10, 2020, https://www.pewresearch.org/fact-tank/2020/06/10/blacklivesmatter-surges-on-twitter-after-george-floyds-death.

32. Kim Parker, Juliana Menasce Horowitz, and Monica Anderson, "Amid Protests, Majorities across Racial and Ethnic Groups Express Support for the Black Lives Matter Movement," Pew Research Center, June 12, 2020, https://www.pewresearch.org/social-trends/2020/06/12/amid-protests-majorities-across-racial-and-ethnic-groups-express-support-for-the-black-lives-matter-movement.

33. Cameron Jenkins, "MyPillow CEO Says Boycotts Have Cost Him $65 Million," *Hill*, February 23, 2021, https://thehill.com/homenews/news/540068-mypillow-ceo-says-boycotts-have-cost-him-65m.

34. Rina Torchinsky, "Days after the Uvalde Shooting the NRA Convention Went On as Planned," NPR, May 29, 2022, https://www.npr.org/2022/05/29/1101994074/nra-convention-houston-ends.

35. Emily Cochrane and Zolan Kanno-Youngs, "Biden Signs Gun Bill into Law, Ending Years of Stalemate," *New York Times*, June 25, 2022, https://www.nytimes.com/2022/06/25/us/politics/gun-control-bill-biden.html.

Chapter 3

1. Ibram X. Kendi, "There Is No Debate over Critical Race Theory," *Atlantic*, July 9, 2021, https://www.theatlantic.com/ideas/archive/2021/07/opponents-critical-race-theory-are-arguing-themselves/619391.

2. Ibram X. Kendi, *How to Be an Antiracist* (New York: Random House, 2019), 23.

3. NAACP Legal Defense Fund, "Natural Hair Discrimination," 2022, https://www.naacpldf.org/natural-hair-discrimination.

4. Aja Romano, "How 'Karen' Became a Symbol of Racism," *Vox*, July 21, 2020, https://www.vox.com/21317728/karen-meaning-meme-racist-coronavirus.

5. Brakkton Booker, "Woman Who Called Police on Black Bird-Watcher in Central Park to Be Charged," NPR, July 6, 2020, https://www.npr.org/sections/live-updates -protests-for-racial-justice/2020/07/06/887809759/woman-who-called-police-on -black-bird-watcher-in-central-park-to-be-charged.

6. Alex Traub, "1955 Arrest Warrant in Emmett Till Case Is Found in Court Base-ment," June 30, 2022, *New York Times*, https://www.nytimes.com/2022/06/30/us /emmett-till-carolyn-bryant-arrest-warrant.html.

7. Judith Ann Schiff, "Pioneers," *Yale Alumni Magazine (Archives)* January/February 2006, http://archives.yalealumnimagazine.com/issues/2006_01/old_yale.html.

8. Brandon Griggs, "A Black Yale Graduate Student Took a Nap in Her Dorm's Common Room. So a White Student Called Police," CNN, May 12, 2018, https:// www.cnn.com/2018/05/09/us/yale-student-napping-black-trnd/index.html.

9. National Academies of Sciences, Engineering and Medicine, "Lessons from a Crisis," April 20, 2020, https://www.nationalacademies.org/news/2020/04/lessons -from-a-crisis.

10. Jamillah Bowman Williams and Elizabeth Tippett, "Five Years On, Here's What #MeToo Has Changed." *Politico*, October 14, 2022, https://www.politico. com/newsletters/women-rule/2022/10/14/five-years-on-heres-what-metoo-has -changed-00061853.

11. Erik Ortiz and Corky Siemaszko, "NBC News Fires Matt Lauer after Sexual Mis-conduct Review," November 29, 2017, https://www.nbcnews.com/storyline/sexual -misconduct/nbc-news-fires-today-anchor-matt-lauer-after-sexual-misconduct-n82 4831.

12. Sarah Whitten, "McDonald's Employees Stage First #MeToo Strike in Chicago, Alleging Sexual Harassment," September 19, 2018, https://www.usatoday.com /story/money/food/2018/09/18/mcdonalds-employees-metoo-strike-sexual-harass ment/1349981002.

13. Malia Lazu, "Why the Critical Race Theory Fight Matters in the Business World," *Banker & Tradesman*, July 11, 2021, https://www.bankerandtradesman.com/why-the -critical-race-theory-fight-matters-in-the-business-world.

14. Tim Reynolds, "Transformative Year: Black Coaches Now Lead 50% of NBA Teams," Associated Press, June 2, 2022, https://nba.nbcsports.com/2022/06/03/trans formative-year-black-coaches-now-lead-50-of-nba-teams.

15. NBC, "Warriors' Steve Kerr Surprises Black Lives Matter Activists in Oakland," NBC Sports, June 24, 2020, https://www.nbcsports.com/bayarea/warriors/warriors -steve-kerr-surprises-black-lives-matter-activists-oakland.

16. DeNeen Brown, "James Madison's Plantation Vowed to Share Power with Black Descendants. Then Things Blew Up," *Washington Post*, April 22, 2022, https://www.washingtonpost.com/history/2022/04/22/james-madison-montpelier-plantation-descendants.

17. Brown, "James Madison's Plantation."

18. Montpelier Staff, "#FreeMontpelier: Updates from the Staff of James Madison's Montepelier," 2022, https://montpelierstaff.com.

19. Gil Kaufman, "No, Lizzo Did Not 'Defile' James Madison's Crystal Flute, Despite How Candace Owens Feels," *Billboard*, September 30, 2022, https://www.billboard.com/music/rb-hip-hop/lizzo-performance-james-madison-crystal-flute-reaction-candace-owens-1235148072.

20. Danielle Kurtzleben, "Top General Defends Studying Critical Race Theory in Military," NPR, June 23, 2021, https://www.npr.org/2021/06/23/1009592838/top-general-defends-studying-critical-race-theory-in-the-military.

Chapter 4

1. Greg Bensinger, "Corporate America Says Black Lives Matter. It Needs to Hold Up a Mirror," *New York Times*, June 15, 2020, https://www.nytimes.com/2020/06/15/opinion/black-lives-matter-corporate-pledges.html.

2. Vivian Hunt, Sundiatu Dixon-Fyle, Sara Prince Partner, and Kevin Dolan. "Diversity Wins: How Inclusion Matters," May 2020, https://www.mckinsey.com/~/media/mckinsey/featured%20insights/diversity%20and%20inclusion/diversity%20wins%20how%20inclusion%20matters/diversity-wins-how-inclusion-matters-vf.pdf.

3. Ben Maiden, "Almost 40 Percent Support JPMorgan Chase Racial Equity Audit," *Corporate Secretary*, May 25, 2021, https://www.corporatesecretary.com/articles/shareholders/32590/almost-40-percent-support-jpmorgan-chase-racial-equity-audit.

4. JPMorgan Chase, "JPMorgan Chase Engages Third-Party for Racial Equity Audit," press release, March 24, 2022, https://www.jpmorganchase.com/ir/news/2022/jpmc-engages-third-party-for-racial-equity-audit.

5. Matthew Schwartz, "In Selma, A 'Final Crossing' for John Lewis across the Edmund Pettus Bridge," NPR, July 26, 2020, https://www.npr.org/2020/07/26/895149942/in-selma-a-final-crossing-for-john-lewis-across-the-edmund-pettus-bridge.

6. George Serafeim, "Social Impact Efforts That Create Real Value," *Harvard Business Review*, September–October 2020, https://hbr.org/2020/09/social-impact-efforts-that-create-real-value.

7. Jason Saul, "Fixing the S in ESG," *Stanford Social Innovation Review*, February 22, 2022, https://ssir.org/articles/entry/fixing_the_s_in_esg.

8. Johnson & Johnson, "Diversity, Equity & Inclusion," 1997–2023, https://www.jnj.com/about-jnj/diversity.

9. Ben Adams, "The Top 10 Big Pharmas for Their Diversity, Equity and Inclusion Efforts in 2022," *Fierce Pharma*, August 1, 2002, https://www.fiercepharma.com/special-reports/top-10-equality-diversity-and-inclusion-pharmas-2021.

10. Sharon Klahr Coey, "Johnson & Johnson Goes Local to Help Black, Hispanic Patients Left Behind by Health Inequality," *Fierce Pharma*, October 26, 2021, https://www.fiercepharma.com/marketing/j-j-launches-challenge-to-help-tackle-health-inequity-six-cities.

11. National LGBT Chamber of Commerce, "2022 'Best-of-the-Best Corporations for Inclusion Named by NGLCC and Partners in the National Business Inclusion Consortium (NBIC)," October 27, 2022, https://nglcc.org/news/2022botbcorporationsnamed.

12. Rosemary Feitelberg, "Black in Fashion Council's First HRC Report Finds Fashion Companies 'Still Unmistakably Devoid of Black Representation," *Women's Wear Daily*, October 1, 2021, https://wwd.com/business-news/business-features/black-in-fashion-council-first-hrc-report-black-professionals-diversity-inclusion1234955146-1234955146.

13. Christina Binkley, "How Ralph Lauren Does Diversity," *Vogue Business*, August 14, 2020, https://www.voguebusiness.com/companies/how-ralph-lauren-does-diversity.

14. GlobalData.com, "Ralph Lauren: Diversity in Workforce in 2022," https://www.globaldata.com/data-insights/consumer/ralph-lauren-diversity-in-workforce-2095835.

15. Tara Donaldson, "Ralph Lauren Only Fashion Company Ranked among 'Best Companies for Women to Advance,'" *Women's Wear Daily*, August 5, 2022, https://wwd.com/business-news/human-resources/paritylist-best-companies-for-women-to-advance-gender-equity-ralph-lauren-1235293837.

16. Ben & Jerry's, "How We Do Business," 2021, https://www.benjerry.com/values/how-we-do-business.

17. Citigroup, "Closing the Racial Inequality Gaps: The Economic Cost of Black Inequality in the U.S.," September 2020, https://ir.citi.com/NvIUklHPilz14Hwd3oxqZBLMn1_XPqo5FrxsZD0x6hhil84ZxaxEuJUWmak51UHvYk75VKeHCMI%3D.

18. Mary Parker Follett, *The New State: Group Organization the Solution of Popular Government* (New York: Longmans, Green & Company, 1920).

19. Matthew Barzun, "There Is a Better Way to Use Power at Work. This Forgotten Business Guru Has the Secrets," *Time*, June 15, 2021, https://time.com/6073304/power-in-the-workplace.

20. Janice Burns, "Are Your Company's D&I Efforts Shallow?," *Harvard Business Review*, May 26, 2021, https://hbr.org/2021/05/are-your-companys-di-efforts-shallow.

Chapter 5

1. Bernice King, Twitter post, April 5, 2017, 9:15 a.m., https://twitter.com/BerniceKing/status/849656699464056832.

2. Tracy Jan, "Pepsi Tried Cashing In on Black Lives Matter with a Kendall Jenner ad. Here's How That's Going," *Washington Post*, April 5, 2017, https://www.washingtonpost.com/news/wonk/wp/2017/04/05/pepsi-tried-cashing-in-on-black-lives-matter-with-a-kendall-jenner-ad-heres-how-thats-going.

3. Todd Henry, *Louder Than Words: Harness the Power of Your Authentic Voice* (New York: Portfolio, 2015), 10.

4. Henry, *Louder Than Words*, 13.

5. Nike.com, "What Is Nike's Mission?," https://www.nike.com/help/a/nikeinc-mission.

6. Julie Creswell, Kevin Draper, and Sapna Maheshwari, "Nike Nearly Dropped Colin Kaepernick before Embracing Him," *New York Times*, September 26, 2018, https://www.nytimes.com/2018/09/26/sports/nike-colin-kaepernick.html.

7. Gina Martinez, "Despite Outrage, Nike Sales Increased 31% after Kaepernick Ad," *Time*, September 10 2018, https://time.com/5390884/nike-sales-go-up-kaepernick-ad/#:~:text=Despite%20the%20backlash%20in,according%20to%20one%20outside%20estimate.

8. Lauren Thomas, "Read Nike CEO John Donahoe's Note to Employees on Racism: We Must 'Get Our Own House in Order,'" CNBC, June 5, 2020, https://www.cnbc.com/2020/06/05/nike-ceo-note-to-workers-on-racism-must-get-our-own-house-in-order.html.

9. John Elflein, "Poverty Rate among People with and without Disabilities in the U.S. from 2008 to 2019," Statistica.com, March 19, 2021, https://www.statista.com/statistics/979003/disability-poverty-rate-us/#:~:text=This%20statistic%20presents%20the%20poverty,disabilities%20were%20living%20in%20poverty.

10. Mark Wilson, "Nike's Hands-Free Shoe Proves That Universal Design Leads to Better Products for Everyone," *Fast Company*, September 21, 2021, https://www.fastcompany.com/90667803/nike-go-innovation-by-design-2021.

11. Max Nisen, "How Nike Solved Its Sweatshop Problem," *Insider*, May 9, 2013, https://www.businessinsider.com/how-nike-solved-its-sweatshop-problem-2013-5.

12. Malia Lazu, "'Banking While Black' Still Happens, Even If You're Famous," *Banker & Tradesman*, March 20, 2022, https://www.bankerandtradesman.com/banking-while-black-still-happens-even-if-youre-famous.

13. Reis Thebault, "He Settled a Racial Discrimination Lawsuit. When He Tried to Deposit the Checks, Police Were Called," *Washington Post*, January 24, 2020, https://www.washingtonpost.com/nation/2020/01/23/banking-while-black.

14. Annie Palmer, "Amazon Fires Two Employees Tied to Staten Island Union Effort," CNBC, May 9, 2022, https://www.cnbc.com/2022/05/09/amazon-fires-two-employees-tied-to-staten-island-union-effort.html.

15. Justin Bariso, "In His First Week Back as Starbucks CEO, Howard Schultz Made a Brilliant Move. It Just May Save the Company," *Inc.*, April 25, 2022, https://www.inc.com/justin-bariso/starbucks-ceo-howard-schultz-how-to-build-trust-problem-solving-emotional-intelligence.html.

16. Jordan Zakarin, "Howard Schultz Says Starbucks Will Never Engage with Union," *More Perfect Union*, June 10, 2022, https://perfectunion.us/howard-schultz-says-starbucks-will-never-engage-with-union.

17. Isabel Vincent, "How Ben & Jerry Rose from Vermont Hippies Selling Ice Cream to Palestinian Activists," *New York Post*, July 31, 2021, https://nypost.com/2021/07/31/how-ben-jerry-rose-from-vermont-hippies-selling-ice-cream-to-palestinian-activists.

18. Traci Rosenthal, "The Real Scoop: How Ben & Jerry's CEO Matthew McCarthy Is Changing the World One Pint at a Time," Columbia Business School, Newsroom, May 19, 2021, https://www8.gsb.columbia.edu/newsroom/newsn/11277/the-real-scoop-how-ben-jerrys-ceo-matthew-mccarthy-is-changing-the-world-one-pint-at-a-time.

19. Combahee River Collective, "The Statement," April 1977, https://combaheerivercollective.weebly.com/the-combahee-river-collective-statement.html.

20. Ashley Lyle, "Nipsey Hussle Explains His Marathon Clothing 'Smart' Store on Crenshaw: 'The Goal Is to Be an Urban Sanrio," *Billboard*, June 22, 2017, https://www.billboard.com/music/rb-hip-hop/nipsey-hussle-marathon-clothing-smart-store-7840863.

21. Erin Evans, "Nipsey Hussle's Commitment Was to His L.A. Neighborhood, Where He Had Big Plans," NBC News, April 2, 2019, https://www.nbcnews.com/news/nbcblk/nipsey-hussle-s-commitment-was-his-l-neighborhood-where-he-n989641.

Chapter 6

1. Inti Pacheco and Stephanie Stamm, "What CEOs Said about George Floyd's Death," *Wall Street Journal*, April 5, 2020, https://www.wsj.com/articles/what-execu tives-said-about-george-floyds-death-11591364538.

2. CEO Action, "Commitment to Diversity and Inclusion Takes All of Us," 2022, https://www.ceoaction.com/purpose.

3. JPMorgan Chase, "JPMorgan Chase Commits $30 Billion to Advance Racial Equity," October 8, 2020, https://www.jpmorganchase.com/news-stories/jpmc-com-mits-30-billion-to-advance-racial-equity.

4. Steven Melendez, "One Reason for the Tech Industry's Great Resignation: Lack of Diversity," *Fast Company*, August 13, 2021, https://www.fastcompany.com/906 65530/great-resignation-tech-diversity.

5. Wiley Edge, "Diversity in Tech: 2021 US Report," 2022, https://www.wiley.com /edge/diversity-in-tech-2021-us-report.

6. McKinsey & Company, "Racial Equity in Financial Services," September 10, 2020, https://www.mckinsey.com/industries/financial-services/our-insights/racial-equity -in-financial-services.

7. Ijeoma Oluo, *Mediocre: The Dangerous Legacy of White Male America* (New York: Seal Press, 2020), 4.

8. Oluo, *Mediocre*.

9. Crystal M. Fleming, *How to Be Less Stupid about Race: On Racism, White Supremacy, and the Racial Divide* (Boston: Beacon Press, 2019), 11.

10. Fleming, *How to Be Less Stupid about Race*, 34.

11. Ayanna Pressley, Twitter post, June 30, 2018, 3:14 p.m., https://twitter.com/ayanna pressley/status/1013184081696346113?lang=en.

12. Robin DiAngelo, *White Fragility: Why It's So Hard for White People to Talk about Racism* (Boston: Beacon Press, 2018).

13. IBM, "Building an Equal Opportunity Workforce," https://www.ibm.com/ibm /history/ibm100/us/en/icons/equalworkforce.

14. IBM, *IBM 2020 Diversity & Inclusion Report*, 2021, https://www.ibm.com/impact /be-equal/pdf/IBM_Diversity_Inclusion_Report_2020.pdf.

15. Lou Maiuri, "What DE&I Means to Me," LinkedIn, October 27, 2022, https:// www.linkedin.com/pulse/what-dei-means-me-lou-maiuri/?trackingId=ORwbv%2 ButTZqQHGRikS51wg%3D%3D.

16. Maiuri, "What DE&I Means to Me."

17. IBM, *IBM 2020 Diversity & Inclusion Report*.

18. Starbucks, "Starbucks to Close All Stores Nationwide for Racial-Bias Education on May 29," April 17, 2018, https://stories.starbucks.com/press/2018/starbucks-to -close-stores-nationwide-for-racial-bias-education-may-29.

19. Christina Brodzik, Melissa Yim, Abigail Leonard, and Jacob Custer, "Using Strategic Communications to Accelerate Your DEI Strategy," Deloitte.com, February 17, 2022, https://www2.deloitte.com/us/en/blog/human-capital-blog/2022/dei-commu nication-strategy.html.

20. Christopher Ingraham, "Three Quarters of Whites Don't Have Any Non-White Friends," *Washington Post*, August 25, 2014, https://www.washingtonpost.com/news /wonk/wp/2014/08/25/three-quarters-of-whites-dont-have-any-non-white-friends.

Chapter 7

1. Harvard School of Public Health, "Black People More Than three Times As Likely As White People to Be Killed During a Police Encounter," June 24, 2020, https://www .hsph.harvard.edu/news/hsph-in-the-news/blacks-whites-police-deaths-disparity.

2. J. Li and L. Karakowsky, "Do We See Eye-to-Eye? Implications of Cultural Differences for Cross-Cultural Management Research and Practice," *Journal of Psychology: Interdisciplinary and Applied* 135, no. 5 (2010): 501–17, https://doi.org/10.1080 /00223980109603715.

3. Boris Groysberg, Jeremiah Lee, Jesse Price, and J. Yo-Jud Cheng, "The Leader's Guide to Corporate Culture," *Harvard Business Review*, January–February 2018, 44– 52, https://hbr.org/2018/01/the-leaders-guide-to-corporate-culture.

4. Kristen Siggins and Kathy Taberner, *The Power of Curiosity: How to Have Real Conversations That Create Collaboration, Innovation and Understanding* (New York: Morgan James Publishing, 2015) 5.

5. Siggins and Taberner, *The Power of Curiosity*, 5.

6. Zach Winn, "Lessons in Innovation Based on the Values of the Cherokee Nation," MIT News Office, November 29, 2022.

7. Charles W. Mills, "White Ignorance," in *Race and Epistemologies of Ignorance*, ed. Shannon Sullivan and Nancy Tuana (Albany: State University of New York Press, 2007), 13–38.

8. Emma Hinchliffe, "The Number of Women Running Fortune 500 Companies Reaches a Record High," *Fortune*, May 23, 2022, https://fortune.com/2022/05/23 /female-ceos-fortune-500-2022-women-record-high-karen-lynch-sarah-nash.

9. Laura Morgan Roberts and Anthony J. Mayo, "Toward a Racially Just Workplace," *Harvard Business Review*, November 14, 2019, https://hbr.org/2019/11/toward-a-racially-just-workplace.

10. Charles W. Mills, "White Ignorance".

11. Hugh Son, "'Appalled'—Here's What Wall Street CEOs Are Saying about the Killing of George Floyd and Protests Rocking US Cities," CNBC, June 1, 2020, https://www.cnbc.com/2020/06/01/wall-street-ceos-speak-out-about-george-floyd-and-protests-rocking-us-cities.html.

12. Stefanie K. Johnson, "What 11 CEOs Have Learned about Championing Diversity, *Harvard Business Review*, August 29, 2017, https://hbr.org/2017/08/what-11-ceos-have-learned-about-championing-diversity.

13. Mary-Frances Winters, 2020, *Black Fatigue: How Racism Erodes the Mind, Body, and Spirit* (Oakland, CA: Berrett-Koehler Publishers), i.

14. Malissa A. Clark, Melissa M. Robertson, and Stephen Young, "'I Feel Your Pain': A Critical Review of Organizational Research on Empathy," *Journal of Organizational Behavior* 40, no. 2 (2018): 166–92, https://doi.org/10.1002/job.2348.

15. Sydney Ember, "Starbucks Initiative on Race Relations Draws Attack Online," *New York Times*, March 18, 2015, https://www.nytimes.com/2015/03/19/business/starbucks-race-together-shareholders-meeting.html?.

16. State Street, "10 Actions to Address Racism and Inequality," https://www.statestreet.com/fr/en/asset-manager/about/our-people/global-inclusion-diversity-equity/10-actions-to-address-racism-and-inequality.

17. Ori Brafman and Rod A. Beckstrom, *The Starfish and the Spider: The Unstoppable Power of Leaderless Organizations* (New York: Portfolio, 2008).

18. Ella Baker Center, "Who Was Ella Baker," https://ellabakercenter.org/who-was-ella-baker.

Chapter 8

1. Azmi Haroun, "New England Patriots Coach Bill Belichick Accidentally Texted Brian Flores to Congratulate Him on NYT Giants Job, Thinking He Was Brian Daboll," *Insider*, February 1, 2022, https://www.insider.com/bill-belichick-accidentally-congratulated-brian-flores-on-giants-job-2022-2.

2. Imani Moise, Jessica DiNapoli, and Ross Kerber, "Exclusive: Wells Fargo CEO Ruffles Feathers with Comments about Diverse Talent," Reuters, September 22, 2020, https://www.reuters.com/article/us-global-race-wells-fargo-exclusive/exclusive-wells-fargo-ceo-ruffles-feathers-with-comments-about-diverse-talent-idUSKCN26D2IU\.

3. Avery Hartmans, "Ex-Wells Fargo Exec Says the Company Held 'Fake Interviews' with Women and People of Color for Jobs Already Filled to Inflate Its Diversity Efforts," *Insider*, May 19, 2022, https://www.businessinsider.com/wells-fargo-fake -job-interviews-diverse-candidates-nyt-2022-5.

4. Charles W. Mills, "White Ignorance," in *Race and Epistemologies of Ignorance*, ed. Shannon Sullivan and Nancy Tuana (Albany: State University of New York Press, 2007), 19.

5. Beth Daley, "3 Ways Black People Say Their White Co-workers and Managers Can Support Them and Be an Antidote to Systemic Racism," *Conversation*, February 2, 2021, https://theconversation.com/3-ways-black-people-say-their-white-co-workers -and-managers-can-support-them-and-be-an-antidote-to-systemic-racism-154052.

6. Curtis Bunn, "Black Women Allege Google Fosters 'Racist Culture' in Lawsuit against the Company," NBC News, March 22, 2022, https://www.nbcnews.com/news /nbcblk/black-women-allege-googles-racist-culture-lawsuit-company-rcna21008.

7. April Glaser and Char Adams, "Google Advised Mental Health Care When Work-ers Complained about Racism and Sexism," *NBC News*, March 7, 2021, https://www .nbcnews.com/tech/tech-news/google-advised-mental-health-care-when-workers -complained-about-racism-n1259728.

8. Glaser and Adams, "Google Advised Mental Health Care."

9. Jamil Smith, "For Toni Morrison, Who Taught Me to See," *Rolling Stone*, August 7, 2019, https://www.rollingstone.com/culture/culture-features/toni-morrison-author -beloved-tribute-868572.

10. KeyCorp., "KeyBank Ranked #23 on DiversityInc's 2021 Top 50 Companies for Diversity," March 10, 2021, https://www.prnewswire.com/news-releases/keybank -ranked-23-on-diversityincs-2021-top-50-companies-for-diversity-301287426.html.

11. Christopher Muther, "Can Boston Get Hip?," *Boston Globe*, June 7, 2012, https:// www.bostonglobe.com/lifestyle/style/2012/06/06/can-they-make-over-boston /KHQLhcBzDLMwUb4S05csUJ/story.html.

12. Muther, "Can Boston Get Hip?"

13. Chris Faraone, "The Fight Continues for Liquor Licenses in Communities of Color," DigBoston.com, January 24, 2015, https://digboston.com/the-fight-continues -for-liquor-licenses-in-communities-of-color/

14. Alicia Adamczyk, "Gen Z Prioritizes Making Money and Having a Successful Career," CNBC, July 18, 2019, https://www.cnbc.com/2019/07/18/gen-z-prioritizes -making-money-and-having-a-successful-career.html.

Chapter 9

1. Exelon Corp., *Built to Thrive: Resilience through Partnerships: 2020 EDBE Annual Report*, https://www.exeloncorp.com/company/Documents/2020%20Exelon%20EDBE%20Report.pdf.

2. Exelon Corp., "Exelon Spent $11.2 Billion with Diverse Suppliers from 2016–2020," August 2, 2021, https://www.exeloncorp.com/newsroom/exelon-spent-$11-2-billion -with-diverse-suppliers-from-2016-2020.

3. MIT Sloan School of Management, "The Inclusive Innovation Economy," September 28, 2021, https://www.youtube.com/watch?v=mXkTIBMrm0g&t=1722s.

4. Alexis Bateman, Ashley Barrington, and Katie Date, "Why You Need a Supplier-Diversity Program," *Harvard Business Review*, August 17, 2020, https://hbr.org/2020 /08/why-you-need-a-supplier-diversity-program.

5. Bain & Company, "Corporate Spending on Diverse Suppliers Rose an Average of 54% In Recent Years, According to New Research from Bain & Company and Coupa," April 28, 2021, https://www.prnewswire.com/news-releases/corporate-spending-on -diverse-suppliers-rose-an-average-of-54-in-recent-years-according-to-new-research -from-bain--company-and-coupa-301278889.html.

6. Radhika Batra, Jason Housh, and David Schannon, "Supplier Diversity: How to Overcome Four Key Obstacles." Bain & Company, April 28, 2021, https://www.bain .com/insights/supplier-diversity-how-to-overcome-four-key-obstacles.

7. Radhika Batra, Jason Housh, and David Schannon. "Supplier Diversity."

8. Target, "Supplier Diversity," n.d., https://corporate.target.com/about/products -services/suppliers/supplier-diversity.

9. Michael Browne, "Target to Spend More Than $2 Billion with Black-Owned Businesses by 2025," *Supermarket News*, April 7, 2021, https://www.supermarketnews .com/issues-trends/target-spend-more-2-billion-black-owned-businesses-2025.

10. Anne D'Innocenzio and Dee-Ann Durbin, "Target on the Defensive after Removing Some Products Aimed at LGBTQ+," May 25, 2023, https://apnews.com/article /target-lgbtq-pride-month-bathing-suits-21393e91a8eb6110b46623d17a3bf507.

11. François Neville, Juanita Kimiyo Forrester, Jay O'Toole, and Allan Riding, "'Why Even Bother Trying?' Examining Discouragement among Racial-Minority Entrepreneurs," *Journal of Management Studies*, October 7, 2017, https://doi.org/10.1111/joms .12319.

12. Karina Swette and Timi Boyo, "Tracking the Supplier Diversity Dollar," 2021, https://www.oliverwyman.com/our-expertise/insights/2021/apr/tracking-the-sup

plier-diversity-dollar.html#:~:text=Many%20organizations%20appear%20to%20
be,program%20report%20supplier%20diversity%20spend.

13. Nate Berg, "More Than 75% of Real Estate Executives Are White Men. Here's
How to Diversity," *Fast Company*, February 17, 2021, https://www.fastcompany
.com/90604991/how-to-diversify-the-very-white-very-male-real-estate-industry.

14. Malia Lazu, "Opening the Door to Great Diversity: A Conversation with Gosder
Cherilus," *Banker & Tradesman*, May 15, 2022, https://www.bankerandtradesman
.com/opening-the-door-to-great-diversity-a-conversation-with-gosder-cherilus.

15. Malia Lazu, "We're Building Black History in Boston," *Banker & Tradesman*, February 20, 2022, https://bankerandtradesman.com/were-building-black-history-in
-boston.

16. Shirley Leung, "City of Boston Spent $2.1 Billion in Contracts over Five Years.
Only 1.2 Percent Went to Black-Owned and Latino-Owned Businesses," February
5, 2021, https://www.bostonglobe.com/2021/02/05/business/city-boston-spent-21
-billion-contracts-over-five-years-less-than-1-percent-went-black-owned-or-latino
-owned-businesses.

Chapter 10

1. Ibram X. Kendi. *How to Be an Antiracist* (New York: Random House, 2019), 218.

2. PBS, *Freedom Summer*, "Searching for Bodies," *American Experience*, 2014, https://
www.pbs.org/wgbh/americanexperience/features/freedomsummer-bodies.

3. FDR Library, June 1941, image gallery, http://www.fdrlibrary.marist.edu/dayby
day/resource/june-1941-9.

4. George Washington University, A. Philip Randolph to Eleanor Roosevelt, letter,
1943, https://www2.gwu.edu/~erpapers/workers/PDF/RandolphER.pdf.

5. Kevin Breuninger, "Kamala Harris Attacks Joe Biden's Record on Busing and
Working with Segregationists in Vicious Exchange at Democratic Debate," CNBC,
June 27, 2019, https://www.cnbc.com/2019/06/27/harris-attacks-bidens-record-on
-busing-and-working-with-segregationists.html.

6. See the website of the Honey Pot, https://thehoneypot.co.

7. Rebecca Russo, "There's Nothing Weird about This Shit': The Honey Pot's Beatrice
Dixon on Demystifying Feminine Health and Wellness," *Glossy*, June 9, 2022,
https://www.glossy.co/beauty/theres-nothing-weird-about-this-shit-the-honey-pots
-beatrice-dixon-on-demystifying-feminine-health-and-wellness.

8. Ben Gilbert, "The Story of Cookies: How a Former Wendy's Employee Turned a
Popular Weed Strain with a Controversial Name into a $1 Billion Empire," *Insider*,

June 8, 2022, https://www.businessinsider.com/the-story-of-cookies-weed-brand-and
-berner-2022-6.

9. Andrew DeAngelo, "Berner: The Circle Is Closed and the Cookies Are Hot," *Forbes*,
October 19, 2021, https://www.forbes.com/sites/andrewdeangelo/2021/10/19/berner
-the-circle-is-close-and-the-cookies-are-hot/?sh=1a39844c3a6c.

Index

Abrams, Stacey, 24
Accountability, 4, 36, 89, 132
Activism, 4, 16, 116
Affective empathy, 95
Affirmative action, 20
Allyship, 34, 74–75, 97, 132–134
Amazon, 62
Antiracism, 28–41, 131
   accountability/visibility, 34–36
   admitting to racism, 32–34
   speaking out, 39–40
   support for policies, 36–39
Apple, 85
Arbery, Ahmaud, 13
Authentic voice, 57–66
   and hypocrisy, 61–62
   practicing, 62–64
   and reputational risk, 66
   sharing, 64–66
   and values, 59–60

Baker, Ella, 102–103
Banking, 61, 84
   CYA behavior, 90
   diversity reputation, 112–113
   and racial discrimination, 78
   and underserved communities, 69,
     73–74
Bank of America, 58, 61, 78
Bastion Companies, 125–126
Beckstrom, Rod A., 101

Belafonte, Harry, 66, 85, 129
Belichick, Bill, 105
Belonging, 31–32, 116
Ben & Jerry's, 51, 63
Bensinger, Greg, 43
Berner, 135–136
Bias, 6–7
   confirmation, 96
   hiring, 105, 114
   historical, 72
   implicit, 30–31
   industry, 58
   institutional, 29–30
   structural, 29–30
Bias to Belonging, 29
Biden, Joe, 25, 134
Big Dig, 124
BIPOC community. See also Black
     people; Hispanic community
   corporate representation, 19
   economic losses, 14, 51–52
   entrepreneurs, 64–66
   exhaustion, 94
   and financial services, 70
   and goal setting, 74–75
   incarceration, 21
   learning about, 97
   overqualification, 92
   scalable solutions, 134
   and vendor diversity, 128
Black Fatigue, 94

Black Lives Matter (BLM), 23, 57–58
#BlackLivesMatter, 23
Black-Owned Business Vendor Fair and
    LatinXpo, 122
Black Panther, 61
Black people
  CEOs, 15
  corporate employees, 19, 87
  cultural racism, 39
  exhaustion, 94
  financially underserved, 69
  health equity, 49
  talent retention, 76, 106
  war on drugs, 21
BlackRock, 91
Boston, 114–116, 126
Boston While Black, 115
Bowman, Jamaal, 23
Boycotts, 24–25
Brafman, Ori, 101
BREATH Act, 23
Brotherhood of Sleeping Car Porters, 133
Brown, LaTosha, 24
Brown, Michael, 23
Bryant, Roy, 30
Buffett, Warren, 22
Bush, Cori, 23
Bush, George, 21
Business performance, 14, 54, 92
Bystander training, 39

Cannabis industry, 135–136
Capitalism, 18–19, 92
Capuano, Mike, 74
Casselberry, Jim, 134
Castile, Philando, 23
Catalysts, 102
CEO Action for Diversity and Inclusion
    pledge, 69
CEOs
  black, 15
  conflicting demands, 18–19
  and DEI work, 34, 91

and diversity, 15, 17, 34
  female, 88, 113
  motivation, 14–15, 26
  and privilege, 54
  promotion opportunities, 117–118
Champions, 103
Chaney, James, 132
Chapek, Bob, 18
Chauvin, Derek, 13
Cherilus, Gosder, 125–126
Cherokee Nation, 86
Chew, Elizabeth, 38–39
Circles, 102
Citibank, 14
Civil rights movement, 19–20
Clark, Malissa A., 95
Clarke, Barbara, 7
Class activism, 22
Clawbacks, 124
Climate change, 4
Clinton, Bill, 21
Coconspirators, 132
Cognitive empathy, 95
Cohen, Ben, 63
Color-blind approach, 20
Combahee River Collective, 64
Community of practice, 131
Confirmation bias, 96
Consumers
  diverse, 54
  preferences, 25, 52
Coogler, Ryan, 61, 90
Cookies, 135–136
Cooper, Christian, 30
Corporate social responsibility (CSR)
    ratings, 121
Corporations. *See also* CEOs; Culture,
    corporate
  accountability, 4, 36
  admitting to racism, 32–34
  authentic voice, 58–59
  and BIPOC companies, 66
  black employees, 19, 87

and boycotts, 24–25
centralized structure, 7–8
and consumer pressure/preferences, 25, 52
DEI missions, 14
and diversity, 16–17, 44
and employee feedback, 52
and equity, 3–4
and innovation, 16
public statements, 67
and racism, 28
and white discomfort, 75
and white privilege, 15–16
Coupa, 121
COVID-19, 16, 23
Critical race theory (CRT), 37
CROWN Act of 2021, 29–30
Cruz, Benjamin, 108
Cullors, Patrisse, 22
Cultural racism, 39
Culture, corporate, 47, 55, 84–103
and business models, 85
culture audits, 91–95
and curiosity, 85–88, 91, 95
and CYA behaviors, 6, 89–91
and decentralizing, 101–103
and DEI strategy, 84
and diversity support, 108
and goal setting, 69–70, 80
and investing, 85
and middle managers, 93
and pushback, 88
and social norms, 72
and talent retention, 116
and 3 L's, 95–99
and vendor diversity, 120–121
and white gaze, 109–110
Curiosity, 85–88, 91, 95, 130
Curley, April, 107–108
CYA culture, 6, 89–91

Daboll, Brian, 105
Dapper Dan, 137

Decentralization, 8–9, 78, 101–103
Deepwater Horizon, 36
Deferred Action for Childhood Arrivals (DACA), 23
Deloitte, 79
DiAngelo, Robin, 75
Dignified Banking Training, 90
Dimon, Jamie, 69
Disabilities, people with, 60
Discovery groups, 8, 52–53, 87
Discrimination. *See* Racial discrimination
Disney, 18
Diversity, 31. *See also* Vendor diversity
and banking, 112–113
benefits of, 44
and business performance, 14, 54, 92
and CEOs, 15, 17, 34
and corporations, 16–17, 44
educating employees, 79
and hiring, 108–109, 113–114
obstacles to, 55
and profits, 44
and pushback, 88
support for, 108
and talent retention, 76
Diversity, equity, and inclusion (DEI)
and belonging, 31–32
bias, 6–7
budgeting for, 94
as business imperative, 10, 46, 56, 71, 123
and CEOs, 34, 91
decentralizing, 8–9, 78, 101–103
goals, 3, 67
holistic nature of, 130
performative, 44–47
pushback, 5–6, 46
scope of, 4
seven stages of, 5–7
support for, 43
and white privilege, 11–12
and work culture, 84

Diversity Wins report, 44
Dixon, Bea, 135–136
Donahoe, John, 60
Donham, Carolyn Bryant, 30
DREAMer movement, 23
Drucker, Peter, 55, 83
Drug education, 20
Du Bois, W. E. B., 136
Dylan, Bob, 26

Eastern Bank, 14
Ecosystems, 131
Ella Baker Center, 102
Ellington, Duke, 136
Empathy, 95–98
Employee resource groups (ERGs), 5, 58,
    77–78, 102
Employee surveys, 52–53, 89
Entrepreneurs, 134–136
Environmental, social, and governance
    (ESG) initiatives, 47–48, 85, 121
Equity
    and affordability, 60
    audit, 45–46
    and belonging, 31–32
    defined, 3
    and DEI funding, 92
    and equality, 32
    and financial services, 70
    and goal setting, 77–78
    health, 49
    and hiring, 4
    real estate, 9
Exelon, 10, 119–120, 129

Facebook, 16
Fair Employment Practices Commission,
    133
Fairness, 92
Fashion industry, 50
Financial crisis of 2008, 21
Financial industry, 134–135
Financial services, 69–70, 78. *See also*
    Banking

Finch, Tom, Jr., 13
Fink, Larry, 91
Fleming, Crystal M., 73
Flores, Brian, 105
Florida, 18
Floyd, George, 12–13, 33, 50, 95
FlyEase clothing, 60
Follett, Mary Parker, 54–56
Forry, Linda Dorcena, 126
Francisco, Paul, 33–34, 98–100
French, James Albert, 38
Fresh Food Generation, 115
Future Boston Alliance, 102, 114–116

Gaetz, Matt, 39–40
Galisgewi, Wahde, 86
Garza, Alicia, 22
Gebru, Timnit, 107–108
Georgia, 24
Glynn, Tom, 126
Goals, DEI, 3, 67
Goal setting, 67–82
    and BIPOC leaders, 74–75
    and bonuses, 77
    and business priorities, 80
    communication, 79–81
    and culture, 69–70, 80
    and employee feedback, 76
    and equity committee, 77–78
    and middle managers, 78–79
    norms and traditions, 72
    preparatory goals, 68–69
    qualitative/quantitative goals, 80–81
    and success, 70–71
    transparency, 124
    and white privilege, 72–74
Golden State Warriors, 37
Goldstein, Susanne, 96
Goldwater, Barry, 20
Goodman, Andrew, 132
Google, 107–109
Greenfield, Jerry, 63
Green New Deal, 22
Greenwood Bank, 65

Gross, David, 65
Gun laws, 25

Hair discrimination, 29–30
Harlem, 136–137
Harris, Kamala, 134
Hassett-Walker, Connie, 12
Health Equity Innovation Challenge, 49
Hennington, Christine, 122
Henry, Todd, 57–58
Hiring
  bias, 105, 114
  commitments, 5
  community networking, 110–112
  and diversity, 108–109, 113–114
  and equity, 4
  and recruiting firms, 113–114
  talent retention, 76, 106–107,
    114–118
  and white gaze, 109
Hispanic community
  financially underserved, 69
  health equity, 49
  and PepsiCo, 71
Historical bias, 72
Hoey, Lynne, 34
Home Depot, 24
Honey Pot Company, 135
Hooks, Benjamin L., 20
Household wealth, 21–22
How to Be an Antiracist, 29, 131
How to Be Less Stupid about Race, 73
Hughes, Langston, 136
Human Resources, 8, 34, 102. *See also*
  Hiring
Human Rights Campaign (HRC), 18
Hurston, Zora Neale, 6, 136
Hussle, Nipsey, 64–65, 137
Hynes, John, III, 126
Hynes, John, IV, 125–126
Hypocrisy, 61–62

IBM, 75–77
Ideology, 102

"I Feel Your Pain," 95
Iger, Bob, 18
Implicit bias, 30–31
Inclusion
  and belonging, 31
  and development, 127–128
  and mission statements, 59
  and profit, 15
Industry bias, 58
Inequality, 29. *See also* Equity
Institutional bias, 29–30
Intention, 16. *See also* Goal setting
Internships, 113
Investing, 85

Jackson, Ketanji Brown, 134, 137
Jackson, L. Duane, 126
Jarvis, Sam, 60
Jenner, Kendall, 57–58
Jim Crow era, 12
Johnson & Johnson, 49
Jones, Doug, 27
Jordan, Michael, 37
Jordan, Vernon, 20
JP Morgan Chase, 45–46, 69
Juneteenth, 96
Just Do It campaign of 2018, 59
Just Say No program, 20

Kaepernick, Colin, 59
"Karens," 30
Karmaloop, 114
Kataly Foundation, 34
Kendi, Ibram X., 28–29, 131
Kennedy, John F., 85–86
"Kens," 30
Kerr, Steve, 37
KeyBank, 112–113
Key business impact and networking
  groups (KBINGs), 112–113
Killer Mike, 65
King, Bernice, 57
King, Martin Luther, Jr., 57, 85, 102–
  103, 129, 133

Known, 134–135
Kodak, 16
Krishna, Arvind, 76

Labor organizing, 62
Ladder to belonging, 31
Latinx community, 49, 69, 71
Lauer, Matt, 36
Learning, 97
Lewis, John, 46
LGBTQIA+ community, 18, 122
Lincoln, Abraham, 11
Listening, 95–96
Lizzo, 39
Louder Than Words: Harness the Power of Your Authentic Voice, 57
Loving action, 98
Lynchings, 12–13

Mabra, Brandy, 15
Madison, James, 38–39
Maiuri, Lou, 76
Major League Baseball, 24
Malcolm X, 137
Marathon clothing, 64–65
Martin, Trayvon, 23
Massachusetts Bay Transit Authority (MBTA), 115
Massport Model, 126, 128
Matthews, Robert, 10, 120
McCarthy, Matthew, 63
Meacham, Jon, 22
Mediocre: The Dangerous Legacy of White Male America, 72
Mentorship, 113
#MeToo, 23, 36
Microaggressions, 3
Middle managers, 8–9, 78–79, 93, 117
Mike, 67–68
Milam, Gilbert, Jr., 135
Mill, John Stuart, 18
Millennials, 17
Milley, Mark, 39–40

Mills, Charles, 6, 11, 14, 88, 106
Minority-owned business enterprises (MBEs), 121, 123–124, 126, 131
Missing Pieces, 97
Mission statements, 59
Mississippi Burning, 132
Mohl, Valerie Red-Horse, 134
Molina Niño, Nathalie, 134–136
Montpelier Descendants Committee (MDC), 38–39
Montpelier plantation site, 38–39
Moore, Ray, 27
Morrison, Toni, 109
Multicultural products, 122
MyPillow, 25
MySpace, 16

National Basketball Association (NBA), 37
National Black Chamber of Commerce, 125
National Football League (NFL), 105
National Rifle Association (NRA), 25
National Trust for Historic Preservation, 38
Netflix, 16
Networks, preexisting, 103
#NeverAgain, 23
Nike, 59–60
Nine-box grid, 117

Obama, Barack, 13, 21
Occupy Wall Street, 22
O'Hanley, Ron, 33, 98–99
Oluo, Ijeoma, 72–73
Organizational empathy, 95–98
Orientation, 114

Pacific Gas and Electric Company, 121
Parkland shooting, 25
Payton, Philip, 9, 136–137
PepsiCo, 57–58, 71
Performative action, 44–47, 54

Phileo, 98
Plessy v. Ferguson, 12
Policing, 12–13
  and education, 20
  NFL protest, 59
  and war on drugs, 21
  and white culture, 83
Poverty, 21, 60
Power of Curiosity, The, 86
Pressley, Ayanna, 74
PricewaterhouseCoopers (PwC), 46
Profits
  and diversity, 44
  and inclusion, 15
Pushback, 5–6, 46, 88

Race, 73
Race Together campaign, 96
Racial discrimination
  and banking, 78
  defense industry, 133
  hairstyles, 29–30
  middle managers, 78–79
Racial gaps, 51–52
Racial segregation, 12
Racism. *See also* Antiracism
  admitting to, 32–34
  cultural, 39
  and goals, 81
  and policing, 12–13
  pushback as, 6
  systemic, 3–4, 28, 55
  and violence, 16
Ralph Lauren, 49–50, 129
Randolph, A. Philip, 133
Reagan, Ronald, 20–21
Reagan administration, 20–21
Real estate development, 9, 125–127
Recruitment, 54, 113–14. *See also*
  Hiring
Redlining, 29
Reich, Robert, 22
Reidy, Bridget, 119

Republican National Committee (RNC),
  20
Reputational risk, 66
Resiliency, 53
Reverse discrimination, 20
Robertson, Melissa M., 95
Robeson, Paul, 66
Rock, Chris, 12
Rockland Trust, 14
Roe v. Wade, 137
Rooney rule, 105
Roosevelt, Eleanor, 133
Roosevelt, Franklin Delano, 133
Roper, Samuel, 13
Runway, 74

Saul, Jason, 48
Scharf, Charles, 106
Schultz, Howard, 62
Schwerner, Michael, 132
Schwerner, Rita, 132
Segregation, 106
Self-Help Credit Union, 74
Selkoe, Greg, 114, 116
Seniority, 88
Serafeim, George, 47
Sessions, Jeff, 27
Settles, Darryl, 126
Seven stages, 5–7
Sexual harassment, 108
Shah, Ushir, 134
Shame spiral, 35
Showing Up for Racial Justice (SURJ),
  73
Siggins, Kristen, 86
Slave patrols, 12
Smith, Adam, 18
Social impact, 48
Souls of Black Folk, The, 136
Southern Tenant Farmers Union, 64
Stakeholder citizens, 53
Starbucks, 62, 96
Starfish and the Spider, The, 101

State Street Corporation, 33–34, 76,
    98–100
Sterling, Alton, 23
"Stop Coddling the Super-Rich," 22
Strategy, 83–84
Structural bias, 29–30
Succession plans, 93–94
Suppliers. *See* Vendor diversity
Surveys, employee, 52–53, 89
Systemic problems, 3–4, 26
Systems change, 67–68

Taberner, Kathy, 86
Talent retention, 76, 106–107, 114–118
Target, 121–122
Taylor, Breonna, 13
Taylor, Richard, 126
TCF Bank, 61
Teasdale, Esperanza, 71
Tech companies, 69–70
10 Actions to Address Racism and
    Inequality, 33, 99–100
Thomas, Sauntore, 61
3 L's, 5, 95–100, 111–112, 131
Till, Emmett, 30
Tometi, Opal, 22
Trump, Donald, 13
Trust, 128
Turner, Kenn, 126
Twain, Mark, 44
Tyson, Mike, 81

Unconscious bias, 30
Unilever, 63
Unionization, 62
UPS, 121
Uvalde shooting, 25

Vector 90, 65
Vendor diversity, 119–128
    best practices, 123–125
    and community building, 127–128
    and corporate culture, 120–121

efficiency, 121
    and industry diversity, 125–127
    supplier spending, 121
    and WMBEs, 119, 124–126
Violence, 16
Voting rights, 24

Waizenegger, Dieter, 45
War on drugs, 21
Warren, Elizabeth, 22
Washington, Donald, 97
Watson, Thomas, Jr., 75
Watson, Thomas, Sr., 75
Wealth gap, 22, 134
Wealth loss, 21–22
Weinstein, Harvey, 36
Wells Fargo, 106
White Fragility, 75
White gaze, 109–110
White ignorance, 14, 88, 90, 106
White privilege, 11, 15–16, 72–74
White supremacy, 73
"'Why Even Bother Trying?' Examining
    Discouragement among Racial-
    Minority Entrepreneurs," 123
Winters, Mary-Frances, 94
Woman- and minority-owned business
    enterprises (WMBEs), 7
    banking services, 14–15
    and underserved communities, 73–74
    vendor diversity, 119, 124–126
Women
    as CEOs, 88, 113
    and GI unemployment, 72
Wu, Michelle, 116

Yale, 31–32
Young, Roy, II, 38–39
Young, Stephen, 95

Zimmerman, George, 23